Is It Possible to Know
We Are Saved?

Written by
Elaine H. Carter

Copyright © Elaine Carter 2018

All rights reserved. No portion of this book may be reproduced, stored in a retrieval system, or transmitted in any form or by any means—electronic, mechanical, photocopy, recording, scanning, or other—except for brief quotations in critical reviews or articles, without the prior written permission of the publisher.

Unless otherwise noted, Scripture quotations marked NIV are taken from the Holy Bible, New International Version®, NIV®. Copyright © 1973, 1978, 1984, 2011 by Biblica, Inc.™ Used by permission of Zondervan. All rights reserved worldwide. www.zondervan.com. The "NIV" and "New International Version" are trademarks registered in the United States Patent and Trademark Office by Biblica, Inc.™ Scripture quotations marked CEV are taken from the Contemporary English Version. copyright © 1991, 1992, 1995 by American Bible Society. Used by permission. Scripture quotations marked KJV are taken from the King James Version. Scripture quotations marked NKJV are taken from the New King James Version®. © 1982 by Thomas Nelson. Used by permission. All rights reserved.

ISBN 0692191100

[ISBN-13 978-0692191101 (Elaine Carter)]

Printed in the United States of America

18 19 20 21 22 [Printer Code] 6 5 4 3 2 1

For more information, write to: ecarter4949@gmail.com

*Dedicated
To*

My mother and father, Roy & Maxine Spradlin, who taught me to trust in God and believe in myself.

Thank you for the blessing of being raised in a Loving and Christian Home.

Table of Contents

1. What Makes Us Doubt That We Are Saved? — 11
2. Have We Been Saved According to God's Plan? — 21
3. What Does Our Relationship with God Tell Us About Our Salvation? — 33
4. Can We Fall from Grace? — 46
5. Are We Keeping Christ's Commands? — 59
6. How Do We Walk in God's Path with Self-Assurance? — 67
7. How Can We Be Open to God's Discipline as a Tool To Make Us Faithful Christians? — 87
8. How Can We Achieve Assurance? — 97

Appendix 1: The Commands of Christ — 113

Appendix 2: The Conversions Recorded in Acts — 123

Preface

I decided to write "Is It Possible to Know We Are Saved?" because I wasn't certain of my salvation, and I needed to have peace of mind, so I could experience joy in my spiritual life. Several of my friends would occasionally express their doubts also. In contrast to our feelings, 1 John 5:13 says we can know for sure that we have eternal life. But how do we know?

To answer that question, we will look at some of the reasons we doubt our salvation and consider scriptures that will help us understand why we doubt and how we can overcome that doubt. Not having assurance makes us easy prey for the enemy to sow seeds of doubt in our heart. Having this assurance will enable us to experience a joyful Christian life, as Christ has promised. We also will look at the importance of keeping Christ's commandments and the bountiful blessings that brings.

This book is only a guide to understanding what the Scriptures say about salvation and living a Christian life. It is a tool to help you study the Word, so you can know and be obedient to the will of God. I urge you to read this book carefully, compare every word to the Scriptures yourself, and think about what God's Word says to you, because He has given us everything we need to know about salvation and Christian living.

The most important decision we can make is to become right with God and His Son, Jesus Christ. The saved are blessed with plentiful living now (as God would have us live), and if we stay faithful until the end, we will receive the reward of a home in heaven for eternity. "We have come to share in Christ, if indeed we hold our original conviction firmly to the very end" (Heb. 3:14).

Through this study I found the assurance and joy I was looking for, and I believe you will too. In the end assurance is a precious gift from God. Let us pray for each other that it will abound among us.

1

What Makes Us Doubt That We Are Saved?

Doubt is a natural part of our lives. We all have doubts about different aspects of our existence, including salvation. Rest assured that such doubts and feelings are normal for Christians. For some, those uncertain times are merely fleeting moments; for some, the uncertainty lasts a long time; and for others, those times define their lives. The Enemy delights in bringing doubts to our minds that cause us to wonder if we are "good enough." Accordingly, Paul said to "examine yourselves to see whether you are in the faith; test yourselves" (2 Cor. 13:5–6). Paul challenged readers to make certain they had truly come to faith in Jesus Christ.

When we first become Christians, we experience a tremendous sense of relief and well-being. The feeling of safety and security is overwhelming. Unfortunately, as time passes and sin creeps back into our lives, most of us occasionally wonder, *Am I still saved?* Since the time I became a Christian, that question has frequently been asked in some form by my friends and fellow church members. Strangely, no one ever gave a decisive or even a reassuring answer. Some said, "I just know it in my heart" or "I love God, go to church, and try to keep His commandments as best I can" or even "I don't believe you can lose your salvation once you are saved." But the most common responses I heard were "I sure hope so" or "I'm about 90 percent sure." I decided I was in that 90 percent bracket, and I realized I needed to know for sure before it was too late. We don't get do-overs. Christians must get it right, because this time is the only time we have.

Is it Possible to Know We Are Saved?

There was a period in my life several years ago when I had fallen away from the Christian principles I had lived by for many years. It started with a troubled marriage and continued as I associated with people who were not Christians, until eventually I became too spiritually weak to do what was right. I knew I couldn't depend on my past years of Christian service for my salvation, and as I looked at the pattern of my present life according to the scriptures, I knew it was not acceptable to God. Fortunately, I had been raised in a strong Christian home, and eventually I began to feel so guilty and fearful that I ask forgiveness of my sins and returned back to Christ. Proverbs 22:6 is really true. "Start children off on the way they should go, and even when they are old they will not turn from it."

But even after I turned back to Christ, I would occasionally have doubts, in part because some of my Christian friends whom I considered to be devout and strong would occasionally doubt their own salvation. These were people who were always helping with church projects, never missing assemblies, and were knowledgeable about the Scriptures. Yet even they sometimes said, "I'm just not sure, but I hope so." I would often think; *how can I be sure if they're not?*

My final realization that I needed to know for sure that I was going to heaven came at my mother's funeral. She had been very sick, and I had gotten the call that she was in her last hours (much sooner than had been expected, I had visited with her only two weeks earlier). I had to travel from Texas to Arkansas, so I rushed back home, praying all the way that I would make it there before she died. I called my brother and asked him to tell her I was on the way and to please hold on for a few hours. Amazingly, she did and when I got there, I climbed in her bed and said my last words to her. I thanked her for being the best mother in the world and said that I would be the best Christian I could be, which, as a Christian mother, was all she had wanted for us kids. She couldn't talk, but I was sure she knew it was me. As she died in my arms, (less than two hours after I arrived) I remember thinking I was present when the angels came to take her soul. It was an incredible experience that I will always hold dear.

My son wanted to speak at her service, and not being able to speak myself, I asked him to read a few words that I had written. I prepared a page of wonderful memories I had over the years and told of how grateful I was that she was my mother. I expressed how much I was going to miss her and finished with "**I will** see you again". At the funeral, as I heard those words read by my son, I had this uneasy feeling. I asked myself *will I see her again, how do I know for sure*? I had to find solid answers. I began studying the Bible to resolve this question definitively for myself as well as other Christians. This book is the result of that study. I want the Bible to speak for me, so we will turn to the Scriptures to answer our questions. As Peter stated, we need to be ready with an answer for anyone who might ask us questions (1 Peter 3:15).

We'll begin by looking at the reasons we doubt our salvation.

Doubt #1: I Haven't Done Enough

I've had some sleepless nights speculating where I would spend eternity, thinking *Is God first in my life? Have I done enough?* Biblical verses regarding our "good works" as Christians are the root of much concern about the current state of our salvation. According to James, some works are required as a manifestation of the faith that exists in the heart or our faith would be "dead."

It seems evident from the scriptures that while good works have their place in the life of the Christian, earning salvation is not one of them. We learn from Paul, in Ephesians 2:8–9 that we can't earn our salvation by works. "For it is by grace you have been saved, through faith—and this is not from yourselves, it is the gift of God—not by works, so that no one can boast." We can add nothing to the accomplishments of Christ on the cross, and therefore only by faith can we be saved. Conversely, James 2:26 states, "As the body without the spirit is dead, so faith without deeds is dead." Faith without works is a dead faith because the lack of works reveals an unchanged life or a spiritually dead heart.

In Romans, 5:1-2, Paul writes, "Therefore having been justified by faith, we have peace with God through our Lord Jesus Christ, through whom also we have obtained our introduction by faith into this grace in which we stand; and we exult in hope of the glory of God." James seems to say just the opposite, "You see that a man is justified by works, and not by faith alone." On the surface this might appear to be a contradiction. People have agonized and argued for centuries, trying to deal with this issue. On closer examination we see James and Paul go together. They don't conflict with each other; they complement each other. Both teach us something vital. Paul looks at what goes on internally; while James talks about the external results. Paul says, "We're saved by faith." James says, "This is what saving faith looks like." Faith is the ground of our assurance and according to James we have assurance of salvation *for* our good works. Good works are the evidence of salvation. As Christians, we should find balance in the faith-versus-works controversy. The two should not be separated.

Paul says that salvation and the good works that follow are entirely of God and that God ordained the process from the beginning. According to Ephesians 2:10, "We are God's handiwork, created in Christ Jesus to do good works, which God prepared in advance for us to do." Therefore, just as we cannot claim any glory for our salvation, we should not claim any glory for ourselves in the good works that follow. Remember also that our good works encourage other Christians (Heb. 10:24). Jesus did all the work of providing salvation, and we respond by demonstrating our love for Him. You might consider it as an outpouring of gratitude just as in our daily lives (in a much smaller way of course) we do good works or acts of kindness for people we love, like bake them a cake, buy them a gift, or mow their lawn. We are outwardly showing our love or appreciation for them.

What Makes Us Doubt That We Are Saved?

While Christians are justified by faith alone, they are not justified by faith that is alone. Are good works a means of assurance for the Christian? Absolutely. We should see them as indicators of God's abiding grace within us. We cling to Christ alone. Then we look at how we are living, examining ourselves and giving thanks to God daily that our efforts and labors continue to assure us that we belong to Christ.

We can see, according to James, some works are required as a display of the faith that exists in the heart or our faith would be "dead." Faith alone saves, but faith that is alone is not the genuine article. It is not saving faith. Salvation must come first, before it can be evidenced in a changed life. So, the question is *"How do our good works play a part in our salvation assurance"*? I believe we will find answers to these questions during the course of this study.

Doubt #2: I Don't Feel Saved

I don't believe we can answer questions about our salvation by relying on our feelings, because they can be deceiving and unreliable. Our feelings can change based on our circumstances, they come and go. Paul—originally named Saul—committed heinous sinful acts by persecuting Christians, yet his conscience never convicted him. Saul hated Christians and made it his goal to capture them and bring them to public trial and execution. Saul was present when the first Christian martyr, Stephen, was killed by an angry mob. He believed he was serving God by jailing and even executing Christians when possible. Acts 23:1 says, "Paul looked straight at the Sanhedrin and said, 'My brothers, I have fulfilled my duty to God in all good conscience to this day,'" indicating that when he was killing Christians, he didn't feel he was doing anything wrong.

Clearly, the feelings in our hearts do not necessarily reflect spiritual reality, and trust in those feelings can easily be misdirected. Proverbs 28:26 says, "Those who trust in themselves are fools." Salvation is based upon what God has said, not on how we think or feel.

Doubt and discouragement, in our Christian lives, are the inevitable result of trying to interpret our feelings as though they were truth. They are not. Whether or not we have doubts does not determine our Christianity. Sometimes doubting can be a good thing. Paul tells us in **2 Corinthians 13:5** "examine yourselves as to whether you are in the faith." Doubts give us an opportunity to test ourselves to be sure that Jesus is truly our Savior and the Holy Spirit is truly in us. A good way to accomplish this is to look at where we are today and compare it to where we were a year ago, are there any improvements?

However, we should guard against doubting ourselves to the point that we just give up on our relationship with God or have a "what's the use" attitude. We need to stop thinking about our feelings and redirect our focus to God and the truth we know about Him from His Word. God is greater than our hearts "therefore, we have boldness toward God." God gives us the confidence to overcome doubts. Our assurance is in Him. Salvation is based upon what God has said, not on how we think or feel. Emotions are not a true measure of our faith.

Doubt #3: I've Been Too Bad to Be Forgiven

Sometimes people lack assurance because they can't accept forgiveness. They are so burdened by their sins that they feel they are too bad to be forgiven, and they think the greater their sins, the more they must do to make up for them. Paul was originally full of wrath for Christ and His followers, full of blasphemy and transgression, and yet Paul was chosen to be God's vessel.

We might ask ourselves, h*ow can I be forgiven while I still commit those sins?* Sometimes it is difficult for us to accept God's unconditional love.

The Devil will try to make us feel guilty even when we didn't do anything wrong. One of the most effective tricks Satan plays on Christians is to convince us that our sins aren't really forgiven, despite the promises in God's Word. Satan constantly reminds us of our past transgressions, and he uses them to convince us that God couldn't possibly forgive or restore us.

But God's Word says, "If we confess our sins, he is faithful and just and will forgive us our sins and purify us from all unrighteousness" (1 John 1:9). What an incredible promise! God forgives His children when they sin if they come to Him with an attitude of repentance and ask to be forgiven. God's grace is so great that it can cleanse sinners from their sins. Even when we stumble, even when we repeat the same sins, we can still be forgiven. We must remember that there is no place we can go that God's grace cannot reach us, and there is no depth to which we can sink that is beyond God's ability to pull us out. His grace is greater than all our sins. Whether we are just beginning to doubt, or we are already drowning in our sins, grace can be received.

That is not to say that a person can sin habitually and continually as a lifestyle and still be considered a believer (1 John 3:7–9). We aren't followers of Christ if we're not walking in the same direction. Paul cautions us to "examine yourselves to see whether you are in the faith" (2 Cor. 13:5).

Doubt #4: God Doesn't Answer My Prayers

Sometimes we lack assurance because we don't think God answers our prayers. Remember, He sees past, present, and future and knows the right time for every answer. He may already be at work on our behalf, arranging circumstances to accomplish His will, opening hearts, and preparing us to receive what He wants to give. Just because things are not going the way we planned that doesn't mean they are not going the way God planned. We should remember not to lose ourselves in the temporary, because God has many things planned for us if we open our hearts and dismiss our doubts. He cannot fail us because He is perfect, and His ways are perfect. "What no eye has seen, what no ear has heard, and what no human mind has conceived—the things God has prepared for those who love him" (1 Cor. 2:9). Too often we pray with expectations of how we think God should work. When He fails to respond according to our timetable and our wishes, we start to doubt. Placing our faith in God and trusting in His good and perfect ways should give us the patience to wait for His answer.

Also, we need to consider that sometimes the answer may be no. Even a no answer will be best for us in the long run. Haven't we all looked back at something we really wanted and prayed for but now are thankful it didn't happen? Both of my sons were football players in high school, and one of them recently told me that he had prayed frequently to be a professional football player. But with what he knows now about head trauma and an NFL player's life expectancy, he is thrilled it didn't work out. Jokingly he added that he could have used the money.

Can We Know for Certain That We're Saved?

Despite all of these doubts, is it possible to know we are saved? The Scriptures say yes, absolutely! "I write these things to you who believe in the name of the Son of God so that you may know that you have eternal life" (1 John 5:13). Also, 1 John 4:13 says, "This is how we know that we live in him and he in us: He has given us of his Spirit." John wrote to assure the church that we can know for certain we are God's children by the way we live our lives *after* we have accepted Christ as our Savior, particularly by our awareness that the Spirit has come to dwell in us through the changes we observe in our lives. Other desirable changes John mentions are:
- We will enjoy fellowship with other believers.
- We will feel separated from the world of unbelievers.
- We will love one another and will abide in Christ.

Being a Christian is not about never sinning but about constantly growing. In that growth we become more resistant to sin, if we allow His Spirit to become the guiding force in our lives.

Peter says if we do these things, we can know that our election is sure:

"For this very reason, make every effort to add to your faith goodness; to goodness knowledge; to knowledge self-control; to self-control, perseverance; to perseverance, godliness; to godliness, mutual affection; and to mutual affection, love. For if you possess these qualities in *increasing* measure, they will keep you from being ineffective and unproductive in your knowledge of our Lord Jesus Christ. But whoever does not have them is nearsighted and blind, forgetting that they have been cleansed from their past sins.

Therefore, my brothers and sisters, make every effort to confirm your calling and election. For if you do these things, you will never stumble, and you will receive a rich welcome into the eternal kingdom of our Lord and Savior Jesus Christ" (2 Peter 1:5–11).

God hasn't hidden anything from us. He has told us what we need to know and do. So, we will explore His Word further and learn how it applies to our lives and specifically to the assurance of our salvation.

Conclusion

The Scriptures clearly articulate a child of God may and should possess a true sense of inner peace and confidence regarding personal salvation. The lack of assurance leads some Christians to assume they are counted among the lost. Such a mistake devastates—breeding inner turmoil and even despair. We should look to Christ for our confidence of personal salvation and we should look to the Scriptures to discern the will of the Lord, finding therein the promise of Christ regarding the assurance of salvation. The life of a Christian must be lived in a spirit of confidence before God, so that Christian virtues can be developed. "Whereby are given unto us exceeding great and precious promises: that by these ye might be partakers of the divine nature, having escaped the corruption that is in the world through lust" (2 Peter 1:4-8).

In the sight of God, assurance of salvation is a virtue. "Therefore, my brothers and sisters, make every effort to confirm your calling and election. For if you do these things, you will never stumble" (2 Peter 1:10). The life of a Christian should be lived in a spirit of confidence before God, so that Christian virtues can be developed. "Through these he has given us his very great and precious promises, so that through them you may participate in the divine nature, having escaped the corruption in the world caused by evil desires" (2 Peter 1:4). The Lord desires that the heart of His people be characterized by joy, which is obtained through our confidence

2

Have We Been Saved According to God's Plan?

Before we continue, it's important to determine if we have truly been saved. Obviously, we cannot have assurance of our salvation unless first we have followed God's simple plan of salvation that is laid out for us in the New Testament. We are told that the Scriptures can make us wise about salvation, that they are inspired of God, and that they will teach us everything we need to know about how to be righteous (2 Tim. 3:14–16).

I like the expression "Jesus wrote the book on salvation" because sometimes it's very difficult to decide what is God's plan and what comes from the world. Even an earnest and sincere seeker of truth would be confused by the religious situation today, with hundreds of denominations, sects, and cults in the United States and other countries. Nevertheless, God has provided adequate instruction to enable us to "recognize the spirit of truth and the spirit of falsehood" (1 John 4:6) if we really want to do so. Just because we *feel* like God thinks a certain way doesn't make it true, we must be in complete agreement with the will of God. These last words of one of Christ's apostles give us a most important rule. The Scriptures are fully inspired, down to the very words, and those who would add to them or take away from them are false teachers. "If anybody is preaching to you a gospel other than what you accepted, let them be under God's curse!" (Gal. 1:9).

I did not realize at age thirteen when I decided to become a Christian what a devastating experience was ahead for me. I was blessed to be raised in a strict and religious home. However, my dad was a devout member of the Baptist Church, and my mother was a devout member of the Church of Christ, and they had many conflicting beliefs. Remarkably, my two older brothers and I were never affected by it. We were conflicted about what was right and wrong until each of us made our decision, based wholly on the Bible. Our parents did an incredible job of teaching us love, righteousness, right from wrong, godliness, and always encouraging us to read the Bible. They never criticized each other regarding religious matters. They read the Bible to us and relayed their opinions about what the Scriptures meant. They differed significantly on important issues, especially regarding how to be saved, if a person could fall from grace, and appropriate music in the church. The three of us alternated each Sunday morning and night, going to church with one parent for the morning services and with the other services that night. It was all very amicable. They even had each other's preacher over for dinner and attended each other's gospel meetings. They never wavered in their personal beliefs but naturally wanted us to follow in their footsteps.

Deciding what I believed and choosing the church that taught those beliefs was a monumental decision for me, because I knew whatever I decided would deeply hurt the other parent. So, my dilemma was deciding which way to go, if either, was right. I had certainly learned enough from the Bible to understand that I, and I alone, would be accountable on Judgment Day for my salvation. It doesn't matter what our parents or friends believe or what the preacher teaches on television. It only matters what the Bible teaches, and it's up to us to search the Scriptures for the truth.

After a lot of Bible study, I concluded from the Scriptures that belief, repentance, confession, and baptism were all necessary to become a Christian. It was in the summer of 1961, when I made my decision. We were having a gospel meeting at the Church of Christ and it was then I knew for certain that I wanted to be baptized and be saved. I told my mother, and naturally she was happy, but she was also sad that I would have to tell my dad. She relayed the story to me that when my brothers had made their decision to be baptized, my dad was working out of town, and he had been upset that he was not home to talk to them. She told me he was in the milk barn and I should talk it over with him. What a long walk—I will never forget it. He was indeed very sad, and he asked only that I stay home that night, and he would read the Bible to me and discuss the process of salvation. He did, and I cried the whole time. How hard that must have been for him. I couldn't sleep that night because of the ordeal I had been through and I was scared I would die and not go to heaven because I wasn't a Christian yet. Even though I know my dad was deeply upset, neither that night nor my decision to be baptized was ever brought up again. We all must make a choice, even doing nothing is a choice. We should study and seek council from the Bible (Prov. 15:22).

I can't stress enough how important it is to read and study for ourselves. In my personal observation, children typically adopt the same religion as their parents without ever questioning its validity.

Towards the end of my dad's life, as the subject of baptism was discussed, he acknowledged that baptism *could* be a key requirement at the time of salvation, but if he were to believe that, he would be going against what his mother and father believed and he was unable to do that.

All of us must read God's inspired Word, the Bible, and be assured that if we do exactly what is said in that Word, we will be saved. The Bible has a lot to say about sin and salvation, and it speaks for itself on this subject. Obviously, our salvation is too important to leave to another person's interpretation, so let's go to the Word of God for the answers. What does the Bible teach about the world's greatest question: What must I do to be saved?

Realize Our Lost Condition

The first thing we must do is agree with God that we are sinful and are separated from Him because of our sin and are subject to His just and holy wrath. "For all have sinned and fall short of the glory of God" (Rom. 3:23). "If we claim to be without sin, we deceive ourselves and the truth is not in us" (1 John 1:8). "Everyone who sins breaks the law; in fact, sin is lawlessness" (1 John 3:4).

Hear the Gospel

We must then hear what God says we must do to be saved. "How, then, can they call on the one they have not believed in? And how can they believe in the one of whom they have not heard? And how can they hear without someone preaching to them?" (Rom. 10:14). You must hear the gospel and then understand and recognize that you are lost without Jesus Christ no matter who you are and no matter what your background is. The Bible tells us that "for all have sinned and fall short of the glory of God" (Rom. 3:23). Before you can be saved, you must understand that you are lost and that the only way to be saved is by obedience to the gospel of Jesus Christ. (2 Thess. 1:8).

Believe

Next, we must believe what God says. "Believe in the Lord Jesus, and you will be saved—you and your household" (Acts 16:31).

"Without faith it is impossible to please God, because anyone who comes to him must believe that he exists and that he rewards those who earnestly seek him" (Heb. 11:6).

"It is with your heart that you believe and are justified, and it is with your mouth that you profess your faith and are saved" (Rom. 10:10).

Have We Been Saved According to God's Plan?

"The jailer called for lights, rushed in and fell trembling before Paul and Silas. He then brought them out and asked, 'Sirs, what must I do to be saved?' They replied, 'Believe in the Lord Jesus, and you will be saved—you and your household'" (Acts 16:29–31).

Repent of Past Sins

Repentance means turning away from sinful desires, thoughts, and actions, rejecting them as shameful and leading to death, and subsequently turning to God (Rom. 6:20–21). Becoming a Christian is more than having a desire to have a relationship with Jesus and asking Him to come into one's heart. We also need to have sorrow for our sins and a desire to live differently as His children.

"In the past God overlooked such ignorance, but now he commands all people everywhere to repent" (Acts 17:30).

"Unless you repent, you too will all perish" (Luke 13:3).

Confess Jesus as Lord

Confession of Christ is a statement made with the *mouth* about *Jesus*. Essentially, we confess Jesus to be all that the Bible claims Him to be. We profess that we believe Jesus to be God's Son, the Savior of the world (Rom.10:9-10). In saying this, we admit that we must live our life in total obedience to Jesus' will. This is what we must understand and intend to convey to others by our confession.

"If you declare with your mouth, 'Jesus is Lord,' and believe in your heart that God raised him from the dead, you will be saved. For it is with your heart that you believe and are justified, and it is with your mouth that you profess your faith and are saved" (Rom. 10:9–10).

"If we confess our sins, he is faithful and just and will forgive us our sins and purify us from all unrighteousness" (1 John 1:9).

Be Baptized for the Remission of Sins

It is our sins that separate us from God. We are to repent and be baptized for the remission of our sins. This is God's instruction on how we solve our sin problem. Only when we submit to baptism as the Lord has commanded, that is for the remission of sins to be saved, do we show our faith in the lord. Only then will He save us.

"Peter replied, 'Repent and be baptized, every one of you, in the name of Jesus Christ for the forgiveness of your sins. And you will receive the gift of the Holy Spirit'" (Acts 2:38).

"This water symbolizes baptism that now saves you also—not the removal of dirt from the body but the pledge of a clear conscience toward God. It saves you by the resurrection of Jesus Christ" (1 Peter 3:21). According to this scripture, it is at the point of baptism, that we pass from an unsaved state into a saved state. In other words, at the time of baptism, we go from being unsaved to being saved.

"Then Philip began with that very passage of Scripture and told him the good news about Jesus.

"As they traveled along the road, they came to some water and the eunuch said, 'Look, here is water. What can stand in the way of my being baptized?' And he gave orders to stop the chariot. Then both Philip and the eunuch went down into the water and Philip baptized him. When they came up out of the water, the Spirit of the Lord suddenly took Philip away, and the eunuch did not see him again, but went on his way rejoicing" (Acts 8:35-39).

Baptism into Christ is a process where the old person dies, and a new person is raised. It is a spiritual birth by which we are given the Holy Spirit. We become children of God by the process of putting on Christ.

"Jesus answered, 'Very truly I tell you, no one can enter the kingdom of God unless they are born of water and the Spirit'" (John 3:5).

Have We Been Saved According to God's Plan?

"Don't you know that all of us who were baptized into Christ Jesus were baptized into his death? We were therefore buried with him through baptism into death in order that, just as Christ was raised from the dead through the glory of the Father, we too may live a new life" (Rom. 6:3–4).

Baptism is the immersion in water for the forgiveness of sins. It is an act of faith and a reenactment of the death, burial, and resurrection of Christ. At this moment Jesus adds the one who is immersed to His church, and the person receives the gift of the Holy Spirit.

You Must Be Faithful Until Death

Once you are saved, God adds you to his church and writes your name in the Book of Life (Acts 2:47; Phil. 4:3). To continue in God's grace, you must continue to serve God faithfully until death. Unless they remain faithful, those who are in God's grace will fall from grace, and those whose names are in the Book of Life will have their names blotted out of that book (Rev. 2:10; Rev. 3:5; Gal. 5:4).

Conversions in the Book of Acts

In my search for scriptures related to salvation, I ran across this chart of conversions recorded in the book of Acts. Acts is not only a book of history but also a book of conversions. If we genuinely want to know what to do to be saved, we can read Acts and find the biblical answer.

Is it Possible to Know We Are Saved?

Matthew 28.18-19	Examples of Conversion				Mark 16.15-16
Preaching	Believed	Repented	Confessed	Baptized	Saved
Pentecost Acts 2.14-41	Believed Acts 2.36	Repented Acts 2.37-38	Confessed Acts 2.47	Baptized Acts 2.38-41	Remission of Sins Acts 2.38-47
Samaritans Acts 8.5-13	Believed Acts 8.12	Repented Acts 8.9-10	Confessed Acts 8.10, 12	Baptized Acts 8.12-13	Remission of Sins Acts 8.16 (2.38)
Eunuch Acts 8.35-39	Believed Acts 8.36-37	Repented Acts 8.36	Confessed Acts 8.37	Baptized Acts 8.38	Rejoiced Acts 8.39
Saul Acts 9.17-18	Believed Acts 22.10	Repented Acts 9.9	Confessed Rom 10.9-10	Baptized Acts 9.18	Sins Washed Away Acts 22.16
Cornelius Acts 10.34-48	Believed Acts 10.43	Repented Acts 11.18	Confessed Acts 10.46	Baptized Acts 10.48	Remission of Sins Acts 10.43, 48
Lydia Acts 16.13-15	Believed Acts 16.14			Baptized Acts 16.15	Faithful Acts 16.15
The Jailer Acts 16.30-34	Believed Acts 16.31, 34	Repented Acts 16.33		Baptized Acts 16.33	Rejoiced Acts 16.34
Corinthians Acts 18.1-8	Believed Acts 18.8	Repented 1 Cor. 6.9-11		Baptized Acts 18.8	Sanctified 1 Cor. 6.11
Ephesians Acts 19.1-7ff	Believed Ep. 1.13; Ac. 19.5,18	Repented Acts 19.18; 20.21		Baptized Acts 19.5 (2.38)	Saved Eph. 2.8-9
Preaching Romans 10.14	+ Faith John 8.24	+ Repentance Luke 13.3	+ Confession Romans 10.9-10	+ Baptism Galatians 3.26-27	= Salvation 2 Timothy 2.10

It must also be noted that baptism is a burial, not a sprinkling (Rom. 6:4). The word *baptism* means to dip, to plunge, or to put under,[1] and it requires sufficient water (John 3:23). Baptism is simply the final act of obedience that puts one into Christ (Gal. 3:27).

Paul's (Saul's) Conversion Story

The conversion of Saul may be the best-known conversion in the New Testament, but also the most controversial. Two important questions need to be asked regarding his conversion: When was Saul saved, and how was Saul saved?

Saul of Tarsus, a Pharisee in Jerusalem after the crucifixion and resurrection of Jesus Christ, swore to wipe out the newly formed believers of "the Way". Acts 9:1 says he was "breathing out murderous threats against the Lord's disciples." On the road to Damascus, Saul was surrounded by a blinding light, and he heard a voice say to him, "Saul, Saul, why do you

---

[1] "Baptize, Baptism," Bible Study Tools, https://www.biblestudytools.com/dictionary/baptize-baptism.

persecute me?" (Acts 9:3-4). When Saul asked who was speaking to him, the voice replied, "I am Jesus, whom you are persecuting. Now get up and go into the city, and you will be told what you must do" (Acts 9:5–6).

The men with Saul heard the sound but did not see the vision of the risen Christ that Saul did (Acts 9:7). Saul was blinded, and they led him by the hand into Damascus to a man named Judas, on Straight Street. (This street is about a mile long and is still in Damascus today.) For three days Saul was blind and did not eat or drink anything.

Jesus appeared in a vision to Ananias and told him to go to Saul. Ananias was reluctant because he knew Saul was a persecutor of the saints. Jesus repeated His command, explaining that Saul was His chosen instrument to deliver the gospel to the Gentiles, their kings, and the people of Israel. So Ananias found Saul at Judas' house, praying, and Ananias laid his hands on Saul, telling him Jesus had sent him to restore Saul's sight and so that he could be filled with the Holy Spirit. Instantly the covering on Saul's eyes fell off, and he could see again. Then Saul was baptized to wash away his sins. Saul ate, regained his strength, and stayed with the Damascus disciples for several days.

The men with Saul on the road to Damascus did not see Jesus, but Saul did. This miracle was meant only for Saul. He witnessed the risen Christ, which fulfilled the qualification for an apostle (Acts 1:21–22). Only those who had seen the risen Christ could testify to His resurrection.

Some say Saul was saved on the road to Damascus when Jesus appeared to him. This can't be true, because after appearing to Saul, the Lord told him to go to Damascus and it would be revealed to him what he must do. When he got there, Ananias said to Saul, "And now what are you waiting for? Get up, be baptized and wash your sins away, calling on his name" (Acts 22:16). So, Saul's sins still had to be forgiven. While he was on the road to Damascus, he was still lost.

This text also reveals *how* Saul was saved. The vision of the Lord had not saved him. His prayers and fasting had not saved him either. He was saved when his sins were washed away in the waters of baptism. This agrees with what Peter proclaimed in Acts 2:38: "Peter replied, 'Repent and be baptized, every one of you, in the name of Jesus Christ for the forgiveness of your sins. And you will receive the gift of the Holy Spirit.'"

We also see from the conversion of Saul what it means to call on the name of the Lord. A person acknowledges Jesus as Lord by being baptized for the forgiveness of sins.

What About the Thief on the Cross?

Another example of a conversion is the thief on the cross, and it has spawned some controversy. Jesus said to one of the criminals who was crucified with Him, "Today you will be with me in paradise" (Luke 23:33), and it is generally accepted that the man was saved. Some people who believe in salvation by faith alone claim the thief on the cross proves that baptism is not necessary.

But note that while Jesus was living on this earth, He forgave people of their sins without requiring all the conditions of salvation that are taught under the new covenant (Matt. 9:2; Mark 2:1–5). Jesus forgave the sins of the paralytic. Read this account closely (Matt. 9:1–8; Mark 2:1–12; Luke 5:17–26). The ones who had faith were those who brought the paralytic to Jesus. It does not say that the paralytic had faith. Can one conclude from this that if the paralytic had his sins forgiven without having faith, then people today can have their sins forgiven without having faith? Of course not (Mark 16:16; Heb. 11:6). Faith is required for an individual to be saved under the new covenant of Christ. Yet Jesus forgave the paralytic without requiring him to have faith.

The same is true of baptism in the case of the thief. To take the view that people can be saved without baptism today because the thief was saved without baptism would mean that people can have their sins forgiven today without faith because the paralytic had his sins forgiven without faith. Neither is true under the new covenant. The new covenant teaches the necessity of both faith and baptism. The thief lived and died under the old covenant. Today we live under the new covenant. The new covenant was not "in force" until Jesus died (Heb. 9:15–17). Therefore, the thief was never under Christ's new covenant command to be baptized. However, after Christ's death, burial, and resurrection from the dead, He commanded all believers to be baptized to be saved (Acts 2:38). Baptism in the name of Christ came only with the death of Christ and the institution of the new covenant. Also, it can't be proven that the thief had not been baptized. John had certainly taught people to be baptized (Mark 1:4; Matt. 3:5–6; Luke 7:30). We do not know whether the thief had heard John preach baptism or if the thief had been baptized by John. To say he was saved without being baptized is to say more than the Bible tells us. But the Bible does tell us that we receive forgiveness only by complying with the terms of Jesus' New Covenant, which does include baptism.

Conclusion

In order to know if we are saved, we must, first and foremost, set in order God's plan for salvation. Christ commanded that the gospel be taught to all nations (Matt. 28:19). He said that after the gospel is preached, people must believe and be baptized (Mark 16:15–16). A great importance was placed upon the preaching of the Word because without hearing God's Word, no one could believe (Rom. 10:14). Christ commanded repentance (Luke 13:3, 5). The apostle Peter preached repentance prior to baptism (Acts 2:38). Christ demanded people confess that He is who He said He is (Matt. 10:32–33) and with the mouth confession is made unto salvation (Rom. 10:10). After hearing, believing, repenting, and confessing comes baptism (Rom. 6:3–5). We can see baptism as the final act in the conversion examples we have in the book of Acts (Acts 2:22–47; 8:4–13). Christ said that if people are not born again of water, they shall not see the kingdom of God (John 3:1–5). God's plan for people to be saved is simple and true. They are taught the truth about Christ and the kingdom (church) (Acts 8:12). Then they become part of the body of Christ through obedience in baptism (1 Cor. 12:12–13).

According to the Bible, the symbolism of baptism declares that three things happen to believers who are baptized: (1) they die with Christ to their old self; (2) they rise with Christ to become a new creature; and (3) they are incorporated in their new life with a living community which looks for the coming of the Lord (Romans 6:1-11). "Then Jesus came to them and said, 'All authority in heaven and on earth has been given to me. Therefore, go and make disciples of all nations, baptizing them in the name of the Father and of the Son and of the Holy Spirit, and teaching them to obey everything I have commanded you. And surely I will be with you always, to the very end of the age'" (Matt. 28:18-20).

After we become Christians, the Bible tells us as a way to grow closer to Christ, we should:

- Tell someone else about your faith in Christ.
- Spend time with God each day. It does not have to be a long period of time. Just develop the daily habit of praying to Him and reading His Word. Ask God to increase your faith and your understanding of the Bible.
- Seek fellowship with other followers of Jesus. We should always work from the basis of supporting each other as Christians.

3

What Does Our Relationship with God Tell Us About Our Salvation?

We can be sure of our salvation and rejoice in the Lord, but first we must know where we stand with God and what is required of us. Amazingly, God has told us in His Word that He wants us to be His children and how to have a parent-child relationship with Him. If you have been blessed by having a loving father and mother who set an example of love and respect for each other and who love their children unconditionally, you will already have a good idea of the *type* of relationship God wants with you. Having a personal relationship with God means including Him in our daily lives by praying to Him and reading His Word in an effort to get to know Him better. We should pray, especially for wisdom (James 1:5), which is the most valuable asset we could have. We should take our needs to Him, asking in Christ's name (John 15:16). Christ is the One who loved us enough to give His life for us (Rom. 5:8), and He is the One who bridged the gap between God and us. We can have a personal relationship with God by putting our faith in Jesus Christ as our Savior. More than anything else, God longs to spend time with us and He wants us to see Him as a God who desires to bless His children. Let's ask ourselves some questions about that relationship.

Do We Follow His Teachings?

Following Jesus means learning to obey Him. What is the point of having a perfect teacher if we do not do what the teacher says? A starting point for knowing and following Jesus is to use every means available to learn more about His teaching. Reading the Gospels is a good place to begin. Jesus said:

> Therefore, everyone who hears these words of mine and puts them into practice is like a wise man who built his house on the rock. The rain came down, the streams rose, and the winds blew and beat against that house; yet it did not fall, because it had its foundation on the rock. But everyone who hears these words of mine and does not put them into practice is like a foolish man who built his house on sand. The rain came down, the streams rose, and the winds blew and beat against that house, and it fell with a great crash (Matt. 7:24–27).

Being a disciple of Jesus is a lifelong journey of conforming ourselves to the image of Jesus and living as He taught. The only way to enter the kingdom of heaven is by *doing* the will of God.

Why Should We Follow Jesus?

Jesus said, "I have come that they may have life and have it to the full" (John 10:10). Jesus can give us an abundant life. He can give us peace with God that passes all understanding (Phil. 4:7). He gives us the Holy Spirit, as He promised, to be our Helper, Comforter, and Guide. He can give our lives a new purpose. Through the Holy Spirit, He can help us overcome the temptations that would otherwise destroy our lives. Jesus can and will do much for us if we follow and obey Him.

But primarily we should follow Jesus because of *who He is*, not because of what He can do for us. We must obey His

What Does Our Relationship with God Tell Us About Our Salvation?

commands because He told us to. Whether we are in a good place or a bad place, we still must follow Jesus, the sovereign Lord of all. Some may think, *I will follow Jesus because He can fix my problems and give me inner peace and joy and a happy home life.* He can do that, but following Jesus can also give us increased trials and persecutions! Remember though, trials are the way that faith is proven, refined, and strengthened. We must focus on following Jesus because He is the Lord of creation, who spoke the universe into existence, who created you and me for His purpose (Heb. 1:2). He is the fearful Lord of judgment, before whom every knee will bow (Rom 14:10–11). He is the gracious and loving Lord of salvation, who gave His life so that all who believe in Him shall not perish but have eternal life (John 3:16).

Following Jesus means we want Him to be the master of our lives instead of trying to run our lives ourselves. We may be tempted not to follow Jesus because we desire worldly comfort and riches, but not following Jesus would mean losing our souls.

If we choose Jesus, He will take us to the Father in heaven. Jesus said in John 14:6, "I am the way and the truth and the life. No one comes to the Father except through me." Jesus is the only way to the Father. That's why being a Christian is so important! Through Jesus we have access to God's love, forgiveness, and truth. He not only taught the truth; He is the truth. Jesus speaks straight about righteousness, godliness, and the judgment to come. He speaks of heaven and God's forgiveness, but He also speaks of hell and God's wrath. Both are important to understand, but only the truth can make us free. That is why we need the Lord and His Word to teach us. We won't find truth by listening to the world.

Examine your relationship with Christ. Are you a follower of Jesus who has denied self and put Him first? Are you proud to own Christ as your Lord, or are you shamed by others into denying Christ? There is no middle ground. Jesus said, "Whoever wants to be my disciple must deny themselves and take up their cross and follow me. For whoever wants to save their life will lose it, but whoever loses their life for me will find it. What good will it be for someone to gain the whole world, yet forfeit their soul? Or what can anyone give in exchange for their soul?" (Matt. 16:24–26). Anyone is you and me! We should follow Jesus because of *who He is*: He is the Son of God, the head of the body, which is the church, and He is our only source of salvation. We should follow Jesus because of *what He has already done* for us: He laid down His life for us because He loved us, He gave His body as a sacrifice for our sins, and He was resurrected to give us victory over the grave. We should follow Jesus because of *what He can do* for us: He can give us true rest for our labors, He can save us from our sins, and He can give us the strength to overcome great obstacles. We should follow Jesus because of *what He will do*: He will come again as Savior for those who are prepared, and He will judge those who have not followed God as unworthy of eternal life.

Do We Have the Desire to Help Others?

One of the marks of a Christian is the desire to help others. It is important to share Christ's love in word and deed. In situations when appropriate, we should also offer an opportunity to hear the gospel. For example, if we were to go into a tragedy-stricken community and start preaching the gospel with no offer to help the sufferers, very few people would be receptive. However, practical help often opens the door for us to share why we do what we do. "What good is it, my brothers and sisters, if someone claims to have faith but has no deeds? Can such faith save them? Suppose a brother or a sister is without clothes and daily food. If one of you says to them, 'Go in peace; keep warm and well fed' but does nothing about their physical needs, what good is it?" (James 2:14–16). We may not always help others perfectly, but if we have been saved, we will desire to help others in need.

What Does Our Relationship with God Tell Us About Our Salvation?

Another way to serve others is to pray for them. Sometimes we forget the power of prayer, but by asking God to help them and provide for them, we can make a real difference in people's lives. We should remember the spiritual and physical needs of others before our own. Also, we should be discreet in helping others. Christ tells us, "When you give to the needy, do not let your left hand know what your right hand is doing, so that your giving may be in secret" (Matt. 6:3–4).

When my oldest brother died, hundreds of people from our very small town attended the funeral. After the service so many people came to our family to tell us stories about the many things he had done to help them over the years. One mother told us that my brother frequently visited her disabled son on Saturdays and helped the family with whatever they might need and even took her son fishing on several occasions. He had done so many kind acts our family didn't even know about. The funeral was a great inspirational lesson on helping others, and I was so proud of him.

Have We Experienced Changes in Our Spiritual Lives?

Our spiritual lives will change with time, we will on occasion grow closer or fall away from the Lord. However, the true believer in Jesus will strive to be led by the Spirit (Rom. 8:14). And if we are led by the Spirit, what fruit will the Spirit produce in us? "But the fruit of the Spirit is love, joy, peace, patience, kindness, goodness, faithfulness, gentleness, self-control; against such things there is no law" (Gal. 5:22–23 NASB). When we have this fruit in our lives, we show people we are Christians by how we act. The fruit of the Spirit is proof that we are becoming more like Jesus, and it characterizes all who truly walk in the Holy Spirit.

Scripture often talks about bearing fruit. Jesus told the story of a farmer who went out to sow seed, and it fell on various types of ground. Some of the ground was rocky or hard. Other ground was receptive, but weeds choked the plants. There was also a portion of ground that was not rocky or full of weeds, and the seed took root. Jesus said this is a picture of the different people who hear the gospel. Those who are true believers bring forth fruit (Luke 8:4–15). We should continually see progress in our prayer lives, in our study of the Bible, and in our service to others. Our willingness to serve is an indication that we are maturing in spiritual qualities. This kind of growth will take effort and intentionality, but it will greatly enhance our spiritual lives and benefit the church. Spiritual disciplines like prayer, Bible study, worship, and service are extremely important parts of imitating Jesus' character. Jesus modeled for us a consistent pattern of spiritual discipline during His earthly ministry.

Do We Bear Fruit?

Spiritual fruit will show itself in our lives as a change in our character and attitude. As we spend time with Jesus through Biblical study and prayer and get to know Him better, we will learn more about His plan for us and become more like Him.

Do others see evidence of good fruit in your life? Remember, we are not given spiritual fruit for our own benefit; we are given that fruit by God for the benefit of others. God uses our words and our actions to exhort, comfort, and edify those around us. Christ is the ground of our salvation, faith is the instrument of our salvation, and works are the fruit of our salvation. Whenever the gospel takes root in our lives, it always produces Spirit-wrought fruit (Gal. 5:22–26). The Spirit enables us to walk in a manner worthy of our calling as Christians (Eph. 4:1–6).

Have you ever met someone and quickly realized he or she possessed these characteristics? I was blessed with a mother and father like that. I grew up with a textbook example of how to be Christlike and profoundly affect other people. I didn't adhere to it all the time, but the groundwork was laid for me,

What Does Our Relationship with God Tell Us About Our Salvation?

and when I got older, it was much easier to incorporate that example into my own Christian life.

If you don't have someone like that in your life, seek out *Christian* friends, spend time with them, learn from them, and let them be your example. Of course, we have the perfect example in Christ and the teachings in the Bible, but we are told to associate with our brothers and sisters in Christ. As we aspire to spiritual greatness, the road is long and hard, and we need all the insight, support, and encouragement we can get. In fact, the Bible insists that we keep company with other Christian men and women and "encourage one another daily, as long as it is called 'Today'" (Heb. 3:13). Spending time with other Christians is truly a great blessing! Remember this: only God and other Christians can truly understand the difficulties you and I face as we struggle to resist the Devil and live faithfully for Jesus.

As is often said, bad company corrupts good morals (1 Cor. 15:33). And Second Corinthians 6:14 says, "Do not be yoked together with unbelievers. For what do righteousness and wickedness have in common? Or what fellowship can light have with darkness?" That doesn't mean we should turn our backs on unbelievers. After all, how else will the love of Christ be shown to them if we don't interact? The key to these friendships is how we represent Christ through our actions and words.

What Is the Difference Between the Fruit of the Spirit and the Gifts of the Holy Spirit?

Please note that the gifts of the Holy Spirit and the fruit of the Spirit are not the same, and it is important that we know the difference. The Holy Spirit, at God's divine choosing, gives certain spiritual abilities, or gifts, to Christians to be used in spiritual service to the Lord—to kindle faith in others and to minister to them. The fruit of the Spirit deals more with *how* a Christian serves the Lord. The gifts of the Holy Spirit are received instantly when a person is baptized into Christ. "Peter replied, 'Repent and be baptized, every one of you, in the name of Jesus Christ for the forgiveness of your sins. And you will receive the gift of the Holy Spirit" (Acts 2:38). The Holy Spirit then produces the fruit of the Spirit, which is a result of the new Christian abiding in Christ. However, the fruit develops gradually.

We can see that Christians have been filled with the Holy Spirit by the gifts that are manifested in their lives. We also know they are living their lives by the Spirit when we can observe the fruit they bear.

We cannot bear the fruit of the Spirit in our own strength. We cannot love, which is the heart of it all, or have joy, peace, forbearance, kindness, goodness, faithfulness, gentleness, and self-control by ourselves. We have no power without the Holy Spirit, who lives in us since we received Christ as our Savior. He gives us the power to show love, joy, peace, and patience. He bears the fruit in our lives.

What better example can we look to for showing the fruit of the Spirit than the ultimate example, Jesus Christ? He perfectly displayed all these wonderful qualities of the Holy Spirit, not only during His earthly ministry, but also during His arrest, trial, and crucifixion. Of course, Jesus was more than just a man; He was God in the flesh. As such, He showed His disciples what can be accomplished through the power of the Holy Spirit, and He instructed the apostles to imitate Him.

"Perfect" Examples of the Fruit of the Holy Spirit

The first fruit of the Holy Spirit listed in Galatians 5 is love. The Greek word Paul used for "love" is *agape*. This sort of love means good will toward others, the love of our neighbor, brotherly affection, which the Lord Jesus commands and inspires. This unconditional love is a fruit of the Holy Spirit. Love characterized Jesus' entire ministry. Of course, the greatest example of that love was the sacrifice He made for all of us. Jesus emphasized the fruit of love during His last supper with

What Does Our Relationship with God Tell Us About Our Salvation?

the disciples. Jesus said in John 15:9–13, "As the Father has loved me, so have I loved you. Now remain in my love. If you keep my commands, you will remain in my love, just as I have kept my Father's commands and remain in his love.... My command is this: Love each other as I have loved you. Greater love has no one than this: to lay down one's life for one's friends."

The second fruit of the Holy Spirit that is listed is joy. Often people question the difference between joy and happiness, but when Paul said joy is a fruit of the Spirit, he was talking about genuine gladness. This joy is a by-product of walking in the Spirit, and it is directly tied to faith in the gospel (1 Peter 1:8). Amazingly, just before Jesus was crucified, instead of thinking of the cruel suffering He would experience, He reminded His disciples that His *joy* would be in them so that their joy would be complete (John 15:11). Jesus reminded the apostles, "I have told you these things, so that in me you may have peace. In this world you will have trouble. But take heart! I have overcome the world" (John 16:33).

The third on the list is peace, and Jesus was a man of amazing peace. One of His titles is Prince of Peace (Isa. 9:6). He referred to this at the Last Supper when He said, "Peace I leave with you; my peace I give you. I do not give to you as the world gives. Do not let your hearts be troubled and do not be afraid" (John 14:27). This is another quality we all need to manifest, especially with all the uncertainty of this life. Jobs are no longer as secure as they were. You never know when the company you work for may be bought out and your job will be gone. Too many marriages end in divorce. We constantly live under the threat of terrorism. With all of this it is easy to lose our sense of peace, even our peace in Christ. Without the peace of God operating in our lives, we could become rattled, shaken, tormented, and knocked off our faith in Christ.

The fourth fruit of the Holy Spirit listed in Galatians 5 is patience. The apostle Paul described this aspect of Jesus' ministry in this way: "But for that very reason I was shown mercy so that in me, the worst of sinners, Christ Jesus might display his immense patience as an example for those who would believe in him and receive eternal life" (1 Tim. 1:16). Even while suffering a painful death by crucifixion, Jesus exhibited the patient endurance to pray for those who were tormenting and killing Him (Luke 23:34). And patience is another quality that is much needed in our fast-paced world. Sometimes it may seem that the patience instilled by the Holy Spirit is the only way we can endure a bad situation.

Kindness, the next fruit on the list, was another trademark of Jesus Christ's ministry. Paul noted this godly fruit when he wrote to Titus, "But when the kindness and love of God our Savior appeared, he saved us, not because of righteous things we had done, but because of his mercy. He saved us through the washing of rebirth and renewal by the Holy Spirit" (Titus 3:4–5). As a result of more people being intolerant and having short fuses, and with everyone always being in a hurry, many people fail to treat others with compassion and respect. A kind word or a kind act to help another person can really do wonders.

When you study the life of Jesus in the New Testament, you can certainly see how kind He was to other people. Jesus was kind to the people who hated Him. He said, "Father, forgive them; for they know not what they do" (Luke 23:34). To ask for forgiveness for others while they are crucifying you shows real love and kindness, perhaps one of the greatest gifts that can be given. When you show undeserved kindness to others you are imitating our Savior. Without question Jesus is the ultimate role model for all of us because He perfectly displayed all the fruit of the Holy Spirit. You cannot help but be more kind to others if God's love is flowing through you.

The sixth fruit of the Holy Spirit in the list is goodness. When Peter summarized the ministry of Jesus, a ministry that he actually witnessed, he stated, "Jesus of Nazareth...went around doing good" (Acts 10:38). And Jesus, speaking of His

What Does Our Relationship with God Tell Us About Our Salvation?

supreme sacrifice, referred to Himself as the good shepherd who gives His life for the sheep (John 10:11). The Bible says the goodness of God will lead sinners to repentance and salvation. Not only does the goodness of God draw people to Him, but this fruit operating in a believer can draw people to God. Spirit-filled saints who possess and display these traits can be like magnets. Many people who have been drawn to Christ say it was because of the love and goodness they saw in a believer. Jesus says we are to carry His light and let that light shine before others.

The next fruit is faith or faithfulness. Jesus had total trust and confidence in the Father, and Jesus was faithful to carry out the responsibilities the Father gave Him. Even though He was in anguish anticipating His imminent crucifixion, He was faithful to the plan of redemption until the very end. He summarized His mission in John 12:27: "It was for this very reason I came to this hour."

Faithfulness is needed in our personal relationship with God and with our friends and families. Once we are saved and have entered into a true relationship with Him, we should cling to Christ and stay faithful to Him for the rest of our lives on earth. Hebrews 11:1 tells us "Now faith is confidence in what we hope for and assurance about what we do not see." Faithfulness includes being full of belief and confidence in God and all that He promises.

The eighth fruit in the list is gentleness. Jesus was incarnated into a human body, but He was a man and God. When we read the Gospels, we should study His actions carefully to see how He engaged with different types of people. At times He set people straight, especially the scribes and Pharisees. But at other times He dealt with people gently, with kindness and love. His actions and behavior toward others should be the greatest example for all of us, and we should pattern our daily walk after Him.

The last fruit of the Spirit listed in Galatians 5 is self-control, the ability to keep one's behavior in check. Jesus, as the

One to whom the Father committed judgment (John 5:22), at any time could have called down enormous power against His enemies. Instead, He exercised self-control throughout His ministry. When Peter tried to take things into his own hands, Christ reminded Peter that if He wished, He could call in "more than twelve legions of angels" (Matt. 26:53), tens of thousands, to deal with those who were abusing Him. Instead, He stayed true to His calling, exercised godly self-control, and allowed Himself to be arrested and crucified.

These are just a few examples of the fruit Jesus Christ demonstrated throughout His time on earth, and He has made it possible for us to yield the same spiritual fruit. As His true followers, we should abide in Him and bear ample fruit. The Bible tells us that our spirit and flesh will war against each other in this life. Our flesh wants immediate self-gratification and will do almost anything to get it. Our spirit knows that some of our fleshly desires are not right, resulting in a tug-of-war between the two. The only way we can limit some of our bodily desires is by developing self-control. Since we live in a very self-centered and materialistic world, many people display poor impulse control. Paul detailed this struggle in Romans 7, and the apostle John summed it up by saying, "our flesh desires to satisfy its lusts" (1 John 2:16). When our spirit is weak, flesh can fulfill its lust resulting in sin (James 1:13-15). Although our desires are strong, the Spirit can bring the flesh under control.

Conclusion

There is no relationship of greater importance, there is no aspect of life any more important, than to know and to become one with God. This is why God gave us Jesus Christ. Undoubtably, sometime in our lives, we will go through difficulties. Maybe even to the point where we start to question everything and wonder why we are in the position that we are in. This is where our relationship with God should come into play. When we have a personal relationship with God, He, through the Holy Spirit, can help guide us through the difficult times.

What Does Our Relationship with God Tell Us About Our Salvation?

Overall a personal relationship with God helps us grow as a person.

You can begin your relationship with God by putting your faith in Jesus Christ as your Savior. You can continue to grow that relationship through continuous, committed prayer and bible study. He assures us: if we ask Him to come into our life He will (Rev. 3:20; Gal.2:20). As you build your relationship with God, your trust and faith are rewarded with spiritual strength, love, knowledge, and peace. "Do not be anxious about anything, but in every situation, by prayer and petition, with thanksgiving, present your requests to God. And the peace of God, which transcends all understanding, will guard your hearts and your minds in Christ Jesus" (Phil. 4:6-7). Share your love with God today and let Him into your heart.

Remember, all things we are to take to God in prayer, recognizing that God is our rock and the source of our life. More than anything else, God longs to spend time with us and He wants us to see Him as a God who desires to bless His children.

4

Can We Fall from Grace?

Once we have confirmed our salvation, do we really have anything to worry about? Can a Christian fall from grace? Are there examples in the New Testament? Have we carefully considered the facts?

The belief of "once saved, always saved" may be one of the most controversial topics of the Bible regarding salvation. It is extremely important for us to know what the Bible teaches.

Throughout the pages of Scripture, grace is portrayed as God's unmerited favor. So then, what exactly is grace? It is His willingness to save us when we don't deserve it. It is His attitude of loving us before we love Him back. Romans 5:8 says, "While we were still sinners, Christ died for us." Therefore, saving grace is the gift of salvation from God, which we could never deserve.

As Christians, we should fill our minds and hearts with the gospel so we are willing to trust our lives to Jesus based on His gift on the cross. That decision, which is faith, gives us access to the grace that flows from Calvary. Salvation comes *by* grace *through* faith. In other words, grace makes salvation possible. And faith is essential in making salvation a reality! Our question then is, can we fall from grace?

The Bible not only warns us to be on guard lest we fail to remain faithful, but it also mentions specific people who did fall. Ananias and Sapphira, members of the Jerusalem church, were stricken in the very act of lying to God (Acts 5:1–11). There was also Demas, one of Paul's fellow workers, who went back into the world (2 Tim. 4:10). The apostle John wrote to the Christians at Ephesus, "You have forsaken the love you had at first" (Rev. 2:5). Simon the sorcerer, who lived in Samaria, was lost, then saved, lost, then saved again (Acts 8:4–24). Even "Judas by transgression fell" (Acts 1:25, NKJV).

The people Paul addressed in Galatians were Judaizers, Jewish Christians. They were children of God who had been set free by Christ (Gal. 3:26; 4:6). But they sinned in that they desired to go back to the Old Testament yoke of bondage and be bound by circumcision. As a result, Christ was of no value to them. They were severed from Christ and had fallen from grace because they were not obeying the truth (Gal. 5:1–2, 4).

Can people receive eternal life if they are severed from Christ and fallen from the grace that saves? "Some have in fact already turned away to follow Satan" (1 Tim. 5:15). The Devil encourages those who once entered the Christian life to defect. The possibility of a fatal and final turning aside by true believers is clearly implied. Would the Devil even bother to tempt Christians if it were impossible to fall from grace?

Peter makes it very clear in 2 Peter 3:17-18 when writing to Christians (brethren) to warn them to be on guard about their salvation. "Therefore, dear friends, since you have been forewarned, be on your guard so that you may not be carried away by the error of the lawless and fall from your secure position. But grow in the grace and knowledge of our Lord and Savior Jesus Christ." Several passages in the Scriptures warn us about the possibility and danger of falling away. Beware lest ye also, being led away with the error of the wicked, fall from your own steadfastness; (Gal. 2:13). The Bible uses different phrases to refer to Christians' actions of falling away from the faith, both in their practices and in God's judgment. Please read the passages listed in the footnote[1] that speak clearly of not only the possibility of falling away but also the impending danger. These warnings would be meaningless if Christians could not fall from the faith.

While the Bible teaches that we can fall from grace, it does not teach that the condition must be permanent. The entire

---

[1] 1 Cor. 10:1112; Gal. 5:4; 1 Tim. 4:1–2; Heb. 2:1–3; 3:12–13; 4:11; 6:4–6; 10:30; James 5:1920; 2 Peter 1:10; 2:2022

book of Galatians confirms this fact because it was primarily written to encourage and call to repentance those who had become estranged from Christ.

Although the idea of once saved, always saved provides comfort and confidence in our salvation, it is an empty hope that deceives its believers into a false sense of security. As with any question or teaching, we must examine the Scriptures to know what is true (Acts 17:11). When we study the Bible, we find numerous warnings against overconfidence and falling from the faith.

One of the most powerful examples of a Christian struggling to remain faithful is the apostle Paul. Considered by many to be one of the strongest and most active apostles, Paul not only felt the danger of becoming apostate himself, he also wrote about it to warn others who were overconfident: "I strike a blow to my body and make it my slave so that after I have preached to others, I myself will not be disqualified for the prize" (1 Cor. 9:27). Shortly after writing this statement, Paul warned those who think they stand to take heed lest they fall (1 Cor. 10:12). The Christians in Galatia had succumbed to a false doctrine that was rampant during the early New Testament era—binding parts of the obsolete Old Testament, such as circumcision, on others. Consequently, Paul cautioned the Christians in Galatia that they had actually fallen away by accepting this false doctrine: "You who are trying to be justified by the law have been alienated from Christ; you have fallen away from grace" (Gal. 5:4). Not only had the Galatian Christians fallen from grace, but they had done so by what might seem to us a small matter. This serves as a lesson to us about God's judgment of those who add to or take away from His Word.

Does God Want Us Back When We Stumble and Fall?

One of my favorite parables, the story of the prodigal son, as told by Jesus in Luke 15:11–32, shows how deep into sin we can fall and still be welcomed back by God. Many believe that the prodigal son represents a Christian who falls away from the truth and then later repents. In this parable a father had two sons, the younger son came to his father to ask for his inheritance. Then he went to a "distant country," suggesting that he wanted to get as far away from his father (God) as possible. The son eventually spent all his inheritance in sinful activities and found himself feeding the pigs, who ate better than he did. He thought of his father, who had servants that lived better than he did, so he "came to his senses" and said, "How many of my father's hired servants have food to spare, and here I am starving to death! I will set out and go back to my father and say to him: Father, I have sinned against heaven and against you. I am no longer worthy to be called your son."

But when the son returned, "the father said to his servants, 'Quick! Bring the best robe and put it on him. Put a ring on his finger and sandals on his feet. Bring the fattened calf and kill it. Let's have a feast and celebrate. For this son of mine was dead and is alive again; he was lost and is found.' So they began to celebrate."

The father had been waiting and watching for the son to come back home, and he recognized his son "while he was still a long way off." God, the Father, desires that none should perish but that all would come to Him through Christ (2 Peter 3:9). The son confessed his sin against the father just as we need to confess our sins to God, because our sins are against God Himself (1 John 1:9; Ps. 51:4; Gen. 39:9). The son acknowledged that he was unworthy to be called the father's son, but the father commanded his servants to bring a robe and to put a ring on his son's finger and shoes on his feet. Finally, the father said to bring the fattened calf and kill it. Then they ate and celebrated because this son had been lost but now was found. The lost son, repenting and enjoying his father's forgiveness, had assurance of his acceptance, without any good deeds to depend on; the older brother, focusing on his good deeds, has no assurance of his acceptance with his father, nor any joy and peace. This lack of assurance will always be present when a person is looking to his/her actions to merit acceptance with God.

Have We Become Careless?

Jesus said, "Be careful, or your hearts will be weighed down with carousing, drunkenness and the anxieties of life, and that day will close on you suddenly like a trap. For it will come on all those who live on the face of the whole earth. Be always on the watch and pray that you may be able to escape all that is about to happen, and that you may be able to stand before the Son of Man" (Luke 21:34–36). Even though we know if we're careless in life, we'll suffer consequences. Even so, we still neglect our physical and spiritual health. In most cases we know the right things to do, but we allow carelessness and our busy schedules to prevent us from doing what is right.

Satan's sole aim is to destroy each of us as Christ followers, and he will do whatever he can to bring this about (John 10:10). But Paul tells us not to give the enemy an opportunity (Eph. 4:27). The Holy Spirit of the Lord Jesus Christ dwells within each of us to guide, direct, encourage, strengthen, and support us as we walk down life's path. We can train ourselves to be mindful and on the alert. Daily we need to reinforce our stand against the tricks of the Devil.

Sin always starts in the mind, so be careful what you see on television, the internet, and social media. Be careful what you hear. Refuse to listen to off-color subject matter. Be careful what you read. These precautions can be a preventive for sin. Matthew 15:19 says, "Out of the heart come evil thoughts—murder, adultery, sexual immorality, theft, false testimony, slander." They are first in the mind, and then they may manifest themselves in overt acts. If the Devil can control your mind, he can control you.

Instead of allowing negative thoughts into our minds, we should fill our minds with good thoughts. Philippians 4:8 says, "Whatever is true, whatever is noble, whatever is right, whatever is pure, whatever is lovely, whatever is admirable—if anything is excellent or praiseworthy—think about such things." We are to renew our minds (Rom. 12:2). In other words, don't become careless, letting your spiritual, emotional, and physical guard down. Be intentional. Stand strong in His truth and promises, seeking to bring Him the glory and honor He deserves. The cross of Christ makes it clear that Jesus was not careless about our souls, and we can't be haphazard and careless about our souls and expect to get to heaven. We know from Scripture that our being ready for the Judgment Day is dependent on our watching and praying. "The faithless will be fully repaid for their ways, and the good rewarded for theirs. The simple believe anything, but the prudent give thought to their steps. The wise fear the LORD and shun evil, but a fool is hotheaded and yet feels secure." (Prov. 14:14–16).

We can learn a great lesson from these Old Testament examples of carelessness and the consequences that followed:

1. Aaron's sons were careless and disobeyed the Lord by burning a different fire before His presence. They served the Lord carelessly and paid with their lives (Lev. 10:1–2).

2. Eli's sons were careless in handling the Lord's offering and abused their God-given position. Because of their carelessness, they lost their lives at a young age (1 Sam. 2:12–17).

3. David and his army were careless in transporting the ark of God without following God's guidelines. As a result, their grand celebration turned into a funeral procession when Uzzah treated the ark irreverently and lost his life (2 Sam. 6:1–7).

God expects us to obey His Word carefully, not carelessly. Unfortunately, carelessness has crept into the body of Christ. Many do not study all of God's Word but want to read only what makes them feel good or supports their way of thinking. Yet throughout the Bible we are taught there are consequences for not obeying God's commands. Sin always has consequences, even if they're not as immediately obvious as in the Old Testament.

When I was young, we lived in a small town in Arkansas out in the countryside with only dirt roads for miles. A county sheriff for years patrolled our area one or two days a week, but we never knew when he would show up. One day my brother was driving on some back roads and came to a stop sign. With no one around for miles he just slowed down, looked, and went on his way. As luck would have it, the sheriff was hiding behind a tree, and with lights flashing he pulled my brother over. As he opened his ticket book, he said, "Ronnie, you didn't come to a complete stop back there at that stop sign." My brother replied, "Well, I nearly stopped." The sheriff said, "Son, do you know the difference between stopping and nearly stopping?" Surprised by the question, my brother said, "What?" He replied, "Twenty-seven dollars and fifty cents!" (It was a long time ago!)

The point is that even the smallest mistakes can have consequences. They don't always show up visibly or immediately. Sometimes they fester as extreme guilt in the sinner. So let us be careful in reading God's Word and obeying it, not adding to it or taking away from it. "I warn everyone who hears the words of the prophecy of this scroll: If anyone adds anything to them, God will add to that person the plagues described in this scroll. And if anyone takes words away from this scroll of prophecy, God will take away from that person any share in the tree of life and in the Holy City, which are described in this scroll" (Rev. 22:18–19). If we are obedient to the Word of God, the Lord will do mighty things through us. God is looking for people who will carefully read and obey His Word.

What Is the "Sin That Leads to Death"?

The apostle John said, "If you see any brother or sister commit a sin that does not lead to death, you should pray, and God will give them life. I refer to those whose sin does not lead to death. There is a sin that leads to death. I am not saying that you should pray about that. All wrongdoing is sin, and there is sin that does not lead to death" (1 John 5:16–17). So then exactly what is a "sin that leads to death"? Does it mean physical death (the separation of the soul from the body) as in the case of Ananias and Saphira, or eternal death (the separation of the soul from God) as in the case of Adam and Eve?

This is a very difficult passage, mainly because it is not clear what John means by "a sin that leads to death". The death spoken of does refer to eternal death, therefore it seems likely John understands there to be at least one unforgiveable sin. Various possibilities for this sin have been suggested, such as the unpardonable blasphemy of the Holy Spirit mentioned by Jesus Himself (Mark 3:28–30). However, most theologians believe "sin that leads to death" is *not* the same as the unpardonable sin (also referred to as blaspheming against the Holy Spirit). Likely this verse refers to people who have come to know Christ (notice this passage is directed to any "brother or sister") and has claimed Him as Lord. They later turned their back on Jesus, totally and continually denying Christ's existence, subsequently becoming apostate. John does not forbid prayer for those living in this sin, but it is evident he doubts whether prayer for them will have any effect.

It should be noted that many have backslidden without becoming apostate. They still believe in Jesus but are living in sin. I believe these are the ones that John is calling on us to encourage and to pray for. John's point is not so much about the "sin that leads to death" but prayer for a brother or sister who sins. In fact, John is so troubled about our sins, and so aware of the fact that Christians can fall into apostasy (fall from grace), that he wants to make certain that God's people are diligently praying for and loving each other. These passages are yet another example of the ability to fall from grace.

In First John, the author is so concerned that our lives reflect our faith in Christ, he devotes two whole chapters (3 and 5) to discerning whether someone is just professing faith or possessing faith. John provides self-examination questions of life, tests designed to give assurance of salvation to believers (5:13 and 1:4; 2:12-14), and to expose those who are non-believers.

What is "Blasphemy Against the Holy Spirit"?

The Scriptures give us an example in Mark 3:22–30 and Matthew 12:22–32. A demon-possessed man was brought to Jesus, He cast the demon out, healing the man of blindness and muteness. The people were amazed. They knew according to scriptures the Messiah had been promised and he would be of the family of David. They said, "Can this be the Son of David?" The Pharisees did not accept Jesus as the Messiah. They thought the Messiah would come as a king and free their nation. "No," they thought "this cannot be the Messiah." They accused Jesus of casting out demons by the power of Beelzebub, the prince of the devils. Jesus knew their thoughts and told them if the demons were cast out by the power of the devil, it would be the devil fighting against himself. And surely, they didn't believe that Satan would fight against himself and destroy his own kingdom. Furthermore, if they were going to say Jesus was casting out devils by the power of Satan, whose power was enabling their *own* people to cast out demons? It was a real dilemma for the Jewish rulers. If Jesus was truly casting out demons by the power of God (which He was), then they were making a big mistake by rejecting Him. This was a very serious matter for them to witness such a miracle and attribute it to the devil! In this situation blasphemy against the Holy Spirit involves accusing Jesus Christ of being demon possessed instead of Spirit filled. This particular type of blasphemy cannot be duplicated today, because Christ is not on earth performing miracles. He told the crowd that anyone who blasphemes against the Holy Spirit "will not be forgiven, either in this age or in the age to come" (Matt. 12:32). Simply put, their sin will never be forgiven.

The unpardonable sin in our world today would be the state of *continued* unbelief, denying the deity of Christ and refusing to come to God through Christ. A definition of blasphemy is insulting or showing contempt or lack of reverence to a deity, to religious or holy persons or sacred things. There is no pardon, either in this age or in the age to come, for any person who rejects Jesus Christ and *dies in unbelief,* no matter what you call it! The choice is clear: "Whoever believes in the Son has eternal life, but whoever rejects the Son will not see life, for God's wrath remains on them" (John 3:36).

There are many sins that are not unto death, but I only know of two sins that are unto death; someone who has become a Christian and falls into apostasy, and someone who denies the deity of Christ by refusing to come to God through Christ (Blasphemy against the Holy Spirit.)

What Are Some Other Objections to Consider?

The Bible tells us that Christians can fall from grace as we've seen in the previous scriptures. However, that doctrine is widely disputed in religion today. Therefore, it's helpful to consider additional scriptures on this topic. John 10:27–29 is often cited by those who claim that one cannot fall from grace: "My sheep listen to my voice; I know them, and they follow me. I give them eternal life, and they shall never perish; no one will snatch them out of my hand. My Father, who has given them to me, is greater than all; no one can snatch them out of my Father's hand."

Is it Possible to Know We Are Saved?

The sheep in this passage are the Christians who are going to heaven, and no one can prevent this from happening. There is no one more powerful than God; no enemy can snatch His sheep from His hand. If we hear and obey the voice of Jesus, then we are part of His sheep, and He will never let us go. Keep in mind that while the Father will never let us go, we can decide to turn our back on the Father and fall from grace as we have seen from so many scriptures. Jesus protects His sheep, so no one can destroy them, *as long as* the sheep hear Jesus and follow Him. But what if they *cease* to hear and follow? Sheep can stray from the shepherd's protection (Luke 15:3–7). Wolves may enter the flock, speak perverse things, and *draw away* the disciples (Acts 20:28–30).

This same idea is conveyed in Romans 8:38–39: "For I am persuaded, that neither death, nor life, nor angels, nor principalities, nor powers, nor things present, nor things to come, nor height, nor depth, nor any other creature, shall be able to separate us from the love of God, which is in Christ Jesus our Lord" (KJV). "If God is for us, who can be against us?" (Rom. 8:31). The answer, of course, is that no one or no thing "shall be able to separate us from the love of God, which is in Christ Jesus our Lord." God, who is all-powerful, cannot fail to provide the heavenly home that He has promised to those who exercise faith and trust in His Son, Jesus Christ. A closer look reveals that God's side of salvation is eternal and that one cannot take away another person's salvation, but it does not teach that the person who has salvation cannot willfully abandon his spiritual life. The continual abiding of Christ in the soul is strictly conditional on the part of the person. If people live by the standard of God's Word and the laws of spiritual life, they will remain saved.

Salvation does not take away our free moral agency (free will), but it leaves us with the power of choice. Adam and Eve, who lived in the best place one could imagine, freely chose to rebel against God when the fruit was presented to them. Being made in the image of God, they had free will, which allowed them the option of rebellion, an option that was provided by the

Can We Fall from Grace?

Devil. Adam fell because he freely chose to disobey God but also because he listened to his wife, who had freely chosen to disobey. It was a choice they both made in full knowledge of what was right and wrong. No one except themselves could have separated them from God. We can choose evil and fall from grace, or conversely, we can accept Christ and choose grace. In other words, salvation involves conditions. Jesus said, "If you hold to my teaching, you are really my disciples. Then you will know the truth, and the truth will set you free" (John 8:31–32). One cannot miss the conditional nature of being a disciple of Jesus Christ: one must continue in His Word. People who teach once saved, always saved also use the term "eternal security." These phrases are never mentioned in the Bible.

Remember that God's love to us is unconditional, but His promises are not unconditional. One of the biggest words in the human language is the little word *if*. And there are some big ifs in the Bible—more than fifteen hundred of them—and more than seven hundred in the New Testament. Here are just a few examples from Jesus:

- "If you forgive other people when they sin against you, your heavenly Father will also forgive you. But if you do not forgive others their sins, your Father will not forgive your sins" (Matt. 6:14–15).
- "If you believe, you will receive whatever you ask for in prayer" (Matt. 21:22).
- "If you hold to my teaching, you are really my disciples" (John 8:31).
- "If you love me, keep my commands" (John 14:15).
- "If you keep my commands, you will remain in my love, just as I have kept my Father's commands and remain in his love" (John 15:10).

As we have seen, God's gifts and spiritual blessings are conditional upon our continued obedience. Sin will always be the righteous person's downfall. We find in the Scriptures that we have a part to play in our continued blessings and relationship with God. We can always depend on God to be faithful, and He will never fail us, but that does not relieve us of our responsibility in the relationship.

Conclusion

The false doctrine, that a child of God cannot so sin as to fall from God's grace and be eternally lost, is a lie of Satan. This same lie was told by Satan in the Garden of Eden to Eve, when he said, "You will not surely die" (Genesis 3:4). Satan told Eve that disobedience to God would not result in death, but it did. This is one of the many lies Satan tells today to cause many people to be eternally lost. Satan wants us to be complacent and not be concerned about being lost. When Satan accomplishes this, he has won the battle. Remember, Satan lived as an angel in heaven with God and then became jealous of God, got into war with Michael and his angels, was thrown out of heaven to this earth, and eventually will be cast into the lake of fire and lost for eternity. Given that, why would we think it is impossible for us, mere humans, to be lost? (Rev. 12:7-9)

5

Are We Keeping Christ's Commands?

With open arms a loving God welcomes all who surrender to His call for a genuine relationship with Him. According to the Bible, obedience to His will is essential. To be sure we know His will, let's take a closer look at Christ's commandments and instructions and particularly at His words to His disciples in His farewell address, where the keeping of His commandments was emphasized again and again.

The commands of Jesus embody much of His fundamental teaching and keeping those commands should be a priority in our Christian journey. Have you ever studied those commandments to determine if you are keeping them? I had not until I started this study. I knew the basics of the commandments, but I now realize there is more to them than loving God (the first commandment) and loving our neighbor (the second commandment) and being the best, most forgiving and helpful person I can be. Some very specific things are listed that I was not doing, like visiting orphans and widows. We all do that occasionally for friends and family, but I think Jesus requires more than that. James said in James 1:27, "Religion that God our Father accepts as pure and faultless is this: to look after orphans and widows in their distress and to keep oneself from being polluted by the world."

The Bible tells us that keeping the commandments of God is proof that we love Him (1 John 5:3). Christ Himself said, "Whoever has my commands and keeps them is the one who loves me. The one who loves me will be loved by my Father, and I too will love them and show myself to them" (John 14:21). In other words, we obey Christ's commands because we love Him, and both God and Jesus Christ will love us.

Keeping Christ's commandments is not only a necessary part of our Christian lives; it should *be* our Christian lives! By carrying out Christ's commandments in our daily lives, we are blessed, and we become a blessing to others in the process. What Jesus said in Matthew 10:8 is important to all Christians: "Freely you have received; freely give." Our ability to live in the love of Jesus, to have power in prayer, and to have a genuine relationship with God is dependent on our compliance with the commandments of Jesus, as cited above. It is not just knowing what they are; it is abiding by them.

For the sake of our love for God and for the sake of our own well-being, we should study and keep the commandments of Jesus Christ. They exhort us not to cause harm to others but, on the contrary, to help them. They teach us how to establish and develop our relationship with God and how to improve ourselves to be "God's best." True obedience, therefore, is giving ourselves entirely to Him and allowing Him to chart our course both in calm waters and in troubled ones, understanding that He can make more of us than we could ever make of ourselves. The Lord's commandments are given out of love and are intended for our joy in this life just as much as they are intended for our joy and exaltation in the next. They mark the way we should act, and more important, they illuminate who we should become.

Here are four scriptures in the New Testament that express the importance of keeping Christ's commandments:

- "If you love me, keep my commands" (John 14:15).
- "Whoever has my commands and keeps them is the one who loves me. The one who loves me will be loved by my Father, and I too will love them and show myself to them" (John 14:21).
- "We know that we have come to know him if we keep his commands" (1 John 2:3).

- "And this is love: that we walk in obedience to his commands. As you have heard from the beginning, his command is that you walk in love" (2 John v. 6).

We are promised that if we obey Christ's commands because we love Him, both God and Jesus Christ will love us. As if that were not enough, many other benefits and blessings come to us through obedience. Obeying the commandments of Jesus will bring rewards beyond measure.

These are some of the blessings Christ promises to us if we keep His commandments.

He promises He will send His Holy Spirit to those who are obedient.

"If you love me, keep my commands. And I will ask the Father, and he will give you another advocate to help you and be with you forever—the Spirit of truth. The world cannot accept him, because it neither sees him nor knows him. But you know him, for he lives with you and will be in you. I will not leave you as orphans; I will come to you" (John 14:15–18).

"Jesus replied, 'Anyone who loves me will obey my teaching. My Father will love them, and we will come to them and make our home with them'" (John 14:23).

"If anyone obeys his word, love for God is truly made complete in them. This is how we know we are in him" (1 John 2:5).

Their joy will become full.

"I have told you this so that my joy may be in you and that your joy may be complete" (John 15:11). Joy comes through obedience to God and to His will for our lives.

Those who are obedient can ask whatever they will, and it will be given to them.

"If you remain in me and my words remain in you, ask whatever you wish, and it will be done for you" (John 15:7). "If our hearts do not condemn us, we have confidence before God and receive from him anything we ask, because we keep his commands and do what pleases him" (1 John 3:21–22). Notice the condition here. If we abide in Him and keep His commandments, our prayers will be answered. The early Christians were able to ask and receive whatever they requested from God. Today we ask but do not consistently receive. Our problem may be our lack of obedience and not necessarily our lack of faith.

In the New Testament we can see that obedience to the Lord's commands was the source of great power, assurance, and joy for those early believers (John 15:10–11; 1 John 3:21–22). Today, God conveys to us through the New Testament that when we keep His commandments, our lives will be happier, and more gratifying. Our challenges and problems will be easier to bear, and we will receive His promised blessings. But while He gives us the commandments, He also gives us free will, which allows us to accept or reject them. Our decisions regarding this will determine our destiny. I believe that a serious study and application of Christ's commandments would be a life-transforming experience and should restore to us the enthusiasm of early New Testament Christianity.

Simply put, keeping the commandments of Jesus is the only way to receive the blessings God wants to give us. Anything else falls short of His requirements and His Word.

When I began to prepare a list of Christ's commandments, I decided to search the New Testament. I stipulate Christ's commandments, because there are many commands in the New Testament that were not actually spoken by Christ. They are all important, sanctioned by God, and should be obeyed, but my focus was on Christ's commandments. It was difficult to identify the commandments in the New Testament, so in my search I may have included some of Jesus' statements and teachings that I construed as commands but were just implied. However, I feel comfortable with my list because I believe we should obey the teachings and instructions of Christ as well. There are disagreements about the actual number of His commands recorded in the Gospels, in part because of the duplications in the four gospels. Also, some commands were intended only for the disciples of that time, and some of the commands were directed specifically at the apostles and would not apply to Christians today. For example, in Matthew 10:7–8 Jesus said, "As you go, proclaim this message: 'The kingdom of heaven has come near.' Heal the sick, raise the dead, cleanse those who have leprosy, drive out demons." Clearly this could not apply to us today.

In my study I quickly discovered that some commands are easier to obey: rejoice, keep your word, pray in faith. Others are more difficult: choose the narrow way, judge not, go to your offenders. And some seem next to impossible: love your enemies and be perfect.

Keeping the commands of Jesus begins with recognizing them. Below is a summary list, and a complete list with the scriptures is recorded in Appendix 1.

1. Repent—Matt. 4:17; (also Luke 13:3)
2. Follow Me—Matt. 4:19
3. Rejoice—Matt. 5:12
4. Let your light shine—Matt. 5:16
5. Honor God's law—Matt. 5:17–19
6. Be reconciled—Matt. 5:23–25
7. Do not commit adultery—Matt. 5:27–30
8. Keep your word—Matt. 5:33–37
9. Go beyond what is ask of you—Matt. 5:38–42
10. Love your enemies—Matt. 5:44
11. Be perfect—Matt. 5:48
12. Practice secret disciplines (giving, praying, fasting)—Matt. 6:1–18
13. Layup treasures in heaven—Matt. 6:19–21
14. Don't let your heart be troubled—Matt. 6:25–26; (also, John 14:27; John 16:33)
15. Seek first the kingdom of God—Matt. 6:33
16. Judge not—Matt. 7:1–2
17. Use discrimination, discern between holy and unholy—Matt. 7:6

Is it Possible to Know We Are Saved?

18. Ask, seek, and knock—Matt. 7:7–8
19. Treat others as you want to be treated —Matt. 7:12
20. Choose the narrow way—Matt. 7:13–14
21. Beware of false prophets—Matt. 7:15
22. Pray for people to spread the Word—Matt. 9:37–38
23. Be shrewd and innocent—Matt. 10:16 (also Rom. 16:19)
24. Fear God, not people—Matt. 10:28 (also Luke 12:4–5)
25. Listen to God's voice—Matt. 11:15; 13:9;13:43; (also Mark 4:23; Luke 14:35)
26. Take My yoke—Matt. 11:29
27. Honor your parents—Matt. 15:4
28. Beware of false teaching—Matt. 16:6, 11–12
29. Deny yourself—Matt. 16:24; Luke 9:23 (also Mark 8:34)
30. Do not look down on little ones—Matt. 18:10
31. Go to Christians who offend you—Matt. 18:15
32. Forgive offenders—Matt. 18:21–22
33. Honor marriage—Matt. 19:4–6, 9
34. Lead by being a servant—Matt. 20:25–28
35. Pray in faith—Matt. 21:21–22; John 15:7
36. Obey the law in civil matters—Matt. 22:17–21
37. Love the Lord—Matt. 22:37–38
38. Love your neighbor—Matt. 22:39
39. Be ready for My return—Matt. 24:42–44
40. Celebrate the Lord's Supper—Matt. 26:26–28
41. Make and baptize disciples—Matt. 28:19
42. Teach disciples to obey My commands—Matt. 28:20
43. Make the church a house of prayer for all nations—Mark 11:17
44. Beware of greed—Luke 12:15
45. Befriend the poor—Luke 14:12–14
46. Be born again—John 3:3–7

47. Keep My commandments—John 14:15
48. Feed My sheep—John 21:15–16

Because keeping Jesus' commandments are critical to maintaining our salvation, an in-depth study of the commandments is needed.

In addition to keeping the commandments listed in the New Testament, we should also give special attention to the Beatitudes (Matt. 5:3–12). Christ gave us the eight Beatitudes in the Sermon on the Mount, recorded for all posterity in the gospel of Matthew. The message of Jesus is positive, speaking of humility and charity motivated by brotherly love. The Beatitudes promise us salvation, not in this world, but in the next, they also describe peace during our trials and tribulations on this earth. These attitudes and virtues were proclaimed by Jesus in His Sermon on the Mount. Most notably, the Beatitudes teach us how to treat other people.

The Eight Beatitudes of Jesus

Blessed are the poor in spirit,
for theirs is the kingdom of heaven.
Blessed are those who mourn,
for they will be comforted.
Blessed are the meek,
for they will inherit the earth.
Blessed are those who hunger and thirst for righteousness,
for they will be filled.
Blessed are the merciful,
for they will be shown mercy.
Blessed are the pure in heart,
for they will see God.
Blessed are the peacemakers,
for they will be called children of God.
Blessed are those who are persecuted because of righteousness,
for theirs is the kingdom of heaven.
(Matt. 5:3–10)

Conclusion

Jesus concludes the Sermon on the Mount by illustrating the benefit of obeying His words. It is not enough to hear them; they must be obeyed. He compares a person who hears and obeys Him to a man who builds his house on a rock. Introducing the Parable of the Two Builders (Matthew 7:21-28), He says, "Therefore whoever hears these sayings of Mine, and does them, I will liken him to a wise man" (verse 24). He then describes this wise man as building his house, that is, his whole life, on the rock of genuine subjection to God. Conversely, the disobedient use unfit material as the foundation of their lives.

Jesus' commandments tell us how to live so we can be His true followers. They are also given to protect us from evil. Jesus made it clear that His commandments are not His but are from His Father, who sent Him. "I have kept my Father's commands" (John 15:10). Keeping the commandments of God is not only a way to show our sincere love for Christ our Savior but the way to eternal life. When asked by a young ruler how to obtain eternal life, Jesus said, "If you want to enter life, keep the commandments" (Matt. 19:17). Jesus confirmed this truth in John 12:50: "I know that his [the Father's] command leads to eternal life. So whatever I say is just what the Father has told me to say."

God who made us all will call us one day into judgment and will require an accounting of how we lived. This is the reason God sent Jesus into the world and has given us the Bible. He wanted us to know why we are here and what is expected of us. Jesus said, "There is a judge for the one who rejects me and does not accept my words; the very words I have spoken will condemn them at the last day" (John 12:48). I am reminded of an old hymn, a favorite of my mother's, that says it well. "Trust and obey, for there's no other way to be happy in Jesus, but to trust and obey."

6

How Do We Walk in God's Path with Self-Assurance?

In addition to warning us against falling away from the faith, the New Testament also provides help to keep us from falling. The first thing we should do to assure ourselves we are being faithful to God is to examine our relationship with Him. We should meet the requirements for growth as a child of God (Acts 20:32; 1 Peter 2:2; 2 Peter 1:5–9). If we are not growing in the faith, we will be falling away from it.

One of our goals in remaining faithful should be to develop a conscience against sin. The Holy Spirit teaches the believer what is right and wrong from the Word of God. The Bible presents to us the truth, and the Spirit enables us to embrace that truth (1 Cor. 2:6–16). The Word will change us, and we will begin to develop convictions against the immoral areas in our lives. The Bible teaches that it is wrong to go against our conscience, but it also clearly teaches that God's Word must inform our conscience.

Paul said, "I strive always to keep my conscience clear before God and man" (Acts 24:16). Paul's conscience was modified by his rebirth as a child of God. As Saul, he persecuted the early Christians because he thought he was serving God. After becoming a Christian, he developed a conscience in line with the righteousness of God rather than the righteousness of man.

So what are we to do if our conscience convicts us that we are sinful? The Bible teaches a clear course of action for our sins:

Is it Possible to Know We Are Saved?

> "If we confess our sins, he is faithful and just and will forgive us our sins and purify us from all unrighteousness" (1 John 1:9).

> "Repent of this wickedness and pray to the Lord in the hope that he may forgive you for having such a thought in your heart. For I see that you are full of bitterness and captive to sin" (Acts 8:22–23).

These passages teach a strong promise from God: if we confess and repent of our sins through prayer, God will forgive us. The very fact that Christians who sin need to ask for forgiveness is another proof of the Bible's truth: sin, both before and after our conversion, separates us from God. If we do not repent in either case, we will forfeit our salvation and God's grace.

We all know someone who is no longer living as Christian, and if we think such a thing could never happen to us, we need to take heed lest we fall! We must stay on guard, knowing that Satan and his forces are constantly trying to deceive us and turn us against God and His truth. We're all vulnerable and at war with a cunning, deceptive enemy.

When we fail to live and worship as God's family, as Christ's Church, we take away from what Christ came to accomplish and damage what He died to establish.

Paul told Timothy to avoid falling away by persevering in God's truth:

> In the presence of God and of Christ Jesus, who will judge the living and the dead, and in view of his appearing and his kingdom, I give you this charge: Preach the word; be prepared in season and out of season; correct, rebuke and encourage—with great patience and careful instruction. For the time will come when people will not put up with sound doctrine. Instead, to suit their own desires, they

will gather around them a great number of teachers to say what their itching ears want to hear. They will turn their ears away from the truth and turn aside to myths. But you, keep your head in all situations, endure hardship, do the work of an evangelist, discharge all the duties of your ministry (2 Tim. 4:1–5).

Conviction from Sinning

Do you feel guilty when you sin? Is there an overwhelming sense that you did something wrong? Genuine believers do sin, but they hate it and fight against it.

On the other hand, people who continue to sin without remorse may need to seriously question their Christianity. Naturally, the more believers sin and the longer they refuse to confess their sins, their hearts continue to harden, and eventually they slide into more and more sin. First John 1:6 states, "If we claim to have fellowship with him and yet walk in the darkness, we lie and do not live out the truth."

Christians should have a strong conviction of sin. If Christ is in us, we will be aware of the difference between good and evil, and we will have a strong desire to please God. We should feel guilty and uncomfortable in the midst of sin, which will drive us back to God. Conviction is one indicator that we belong to the Lord.

Jesus said that the Advocate, the Holy Spirit, will come into believers' lives and convict them when they sin: "But very truly I tell you, it is for your good that I am going away. Unless I go away, the Advocate will not come to you; but if I go, I will send him to you. When he comes, he will prove the world to be in the wrong about sin and righteousness and judgment" (John 16:7–8). Every believer will still sin, but when we sin, we will feel conviction from God the Holy Spirit and will want to confess to God. Christians' desires are transformed, and they begin to hate sin and love righteousness (Heb. 1:9). The Psalmist David said, "You who love the Lord, hate evil!" (Ps. 97:10). No

Christian will be sinless, but the pattern of the Christian's life will be decreasing in sin and increasing in righteousness.

Loving One Another

Can a Christian claim to be saved and yet hate a brother or sister? On the contrary, loving other Christians is another important indicator that we will want to see in ourselves. "We know that we have passed from death to life, because we love each other. Anyone who does not love remains in death" (1 John 3:14). No one can hate their brother or sister in Christ and claim to be a believer. Jesus said a strong indication of believers is that they love each other: "A new command I give you: Love one another. As I have loved you, so you must love one another. By this everyone will know that you are my disciples, if you love one another" (John 13:34–35). An important phrase in these verses is "by this." Jesus is saying that by our love for one another, everyone will know that we are His disciples. Loving one another tells believers and nonbelievers that we belong to Christ.

Abstaining from Sin

Christians will still sin, but they do not remain in sin or keep on sinning as if nothing is wrong. Many who have confessed to be Christians live in ways that are contrary to the ways of God. John stated a serious warning to those who think they are saved but feel no conviction of continual sin (1 John 3:6).

The Scriptures make it clear that we are always responsible for our choices because God continuously provides a way of escape from temptation. "No temptation has overtaken you except what is common to mankind. And God is faithful; He will not let you be tempted beyond what you can bear. But when you are tempted, He will also provide a way out so that you can endure it" (1 Cor. 10:13). A way out is a promise. Our task is to look for it and accept it, whatever the cost. God's people will stumble and sin, but we must grow in obedience and repentance. However, if we make a practice of disobedience without repentance, then we are rejecting what Jesus did for us.

First John 3:6–10 says: "No one who lives in Him keeps on sinning. No one who continues to sin has either seen Him or known Him. Dear children do not let anyone lead you astray. The one who does what is right is righteous, just as he is righteous. The one who does what is sinful is of the devil, because the devil has been sinning from the beginning. The reason the Son of God appeared was to destroy the devil's work. No one who is born of God will continue to sin, because God's seed remains in them; they cannot go on sinning, because they have been born of God. This is how we know who the children of God are and who the children of the devil are: Anyone who does not do what is right is not God's child, nor is anyone who does not love their brother and sister."

Reading the Bible Regularly

Can you imagine how God must feel when we read His word only on Sunday or in church? God has sent us the greatest books ever written, sixty-six of them, and these books show us His unconditional love, a love so deep He sent His only Son to die for us. By not reading the Bible and not praying regularly, we demonstrate that God is not first in our lives.

There is an old witticism that can, unfortunately, hit home with us from time to time: A little girl found a Bible in the corner of the house. She held it up and asked her mother, "What book is this, mother?" She replied, "That is God's book, the Bible." The little girl, with piercing insight, advised, "Why don't we send it back to Him, since we never use it?" The truth is that even if we read the Bible every day and still fail to apply it, we would accomplish nothing. When we become what the Bible teaches us to be, only then are we making the proper use of it. Also, a promise is made with regard to Bible study, "more of our prayers will be answered". "If you remain in me and my words remain in you, ask whatever you wish, and it will be done for you" John 15:7.

Paul said, "Do your best to present yourself to God as one approved, a worker who does not need to be ashamed and who correctly handles the word of truth" (2 Tim. 2:15). It is essential for those who make up the church to study the Bible. Christians must search the Scriptures, so they may know the Lord and be able to please Him. "To the Jews who had believed Him, Jesus said, 'If you hold to my teaching, you are really my disciples. Then you will know the truth, and the truth will set you free'" (John 8:31–32). The Bible reveals God's will to people so that we may worship and serve God acceptably. Those who stay faithful will study God's Word in order to grow in faith and the knowledge of Jesus Christ.

I read a funny story of a man who lived far away from his girlfriend. He wanted to marry her, so he wrote her letters all the time but never visited her or called her on the phone. After dozens of letters over a period of years, do you know what this woman did? She married the postal carrier! This may not be a true story, but it makes a good point. Our relationship with God should be a two-way street, and communication is key. In fact, Christians should feel a strong need to read the Bible to know Jesus better and what He would have us do. Only Jesus can satisfy this deep thirst. As He said, "Whoever drinks the water I give them will never thirst. Indeed, the water I give them will become in them a spring of water welling up to eternal life" (John 4:14).

Praying Regularly

Prayer is a way for Christians to relate their feelings, emotions, and desires to God. Jesus prayed to God so often that His disciples asked Him to teach them how to pray (Luke 11:1). I am concerned that our tendency is to pray to God only when we are in trouble or when we decide we can't handle something by ourselves. We should set a daily routine for prayer and Bible study, because this is our channel to God.

For years, before my brother died, he set aside about forty-five minutes every day to go into a room and pray privately. Do you know how hard it is to pray continually for forty-five minutes? I always admired him so much, and there was a standing assumption in our family that if we had a serious problem or really needed something, we asked him to pray about it. James 5:16 says, "The prayer of a righteous person is powerful and effective," and Matthew 6:6 states, "But when you pray, go into your room, close the door and pray to your Father, who is unseen. Then your Father, who sees what is done in secret, will reward you." Prayer should be daily, sincere, fervent, and real. Just as Christians need daily bread, we also need daily prayer. "Do not be anxious about anything, but in every situation, by prayer and petition, with thanksgiving, present your requests to God. And the peace of God, which transcends all understanding, will guard your hearts and your minds in Christ Jesus" (Phil. 4:6–7). God's people must be praying people.

What is Meant by "Pray Continually"?

First Thessalonians 5:16–18 says, "Rejoice always, pray continually, give thanks in all circumstances; for this is God's will for you in Christ Jesus." Is it really possible to pray continually and to give thanks in all circumstances? Obviously it cannot mean we are to keep our heads bowed all day long. Paul is not referring to nonstop talking to God but rather to an attitude of God consciousness that we carry with us all the time. Every waking moment is to be lived in an awareness that God is with us and that He is actively involved and engaged in our thoughts and actions. We can think of situations in which it would be really difficult, but the Bible teaches us that through Christ it is possible to maintain a spirit of praise and thankfulness even in the most trying circumstances. God speaks to us through the Bible. We speak to Him through prayer. In prayer, we make our thoughts known to the mind of God. No matter how much good we do, or how much we study God's Word, we still need

His care and protection. Prayer is an important part of a Christian's life. It is one of the blessings of being in Christ (Ephesians 1:3).

Should We Attend All Church Services?

The writer of the Hebrew epistle tells us not to forsake assembling together: "And let us consider how we may spur one another on toward love and good deeds, not giving up meeting together, as some are in the habit of doing, but encouraging one another—and all the more as you see the Day approaching" (10:24–25). This passage is an exhortation and a warning for Christians to not forsake the assembly as some habitually do. It's interesting that, even in the early church, there were those who made a "habit" of not fellowshipping with other believers. Their example is not to be followed. The church is where our spiritual gifts best edify the Body of Christ (Eph. 4:11–12), and it is difficult to "spur" each other to love and good works if we are not attending church. Christians should be *committed, involved, and supportive* to their local congregation. This requires regular church attendance. A believer will naturally love his brothers and sisters in Christ (1 John 4:21), and that love will manifest itself in a desire to fellowship, not avoidance.

Why should the church meet? In addition to receiving the preaching and teaching of the Word of God that increases our faith and builds us up spiritually, we come together with pure hearts to worship and study. We grow closer to one another and encourage one another as we draw closer to God. We also grow spiritually as we interact with other believers. We learn humility, gentleness, and patience, developing the character of Christ as we relate within the body of Christ. Additionally, there is the promise of the Lord's presence whenever two or more gather specifically in the name of Jesus (Matt. 18:20).

If we need one more reason to go to church, we can look at Jesus Christ, our living example. He went to the synagogue as a regular practice. Luke 4:16 says, "He went to Nazareth, where he had been brought up, and on the Sabbath day he went into the synagogue, as was his custom." It was Jesus' custom, His regular practice, to go to the synagogue. If Jesus made it a priority to meet with other believers, shouldn't we, as Christians, do the same? Each child of God should have the attitude of David, who said, "I rejoiced with those who said to me, 'Let us go to the house of the LORD'" (Ps. 122:1). We need a conscious break from work, family problems, and self-interests so we can concentrate on the Lord. We should make plans to be at every service. Additionally, going to church is an expression of our love for God, and it honors the Lord's Day. Most important, going to church is a matter of obeying God's Word.

Seeking Those Who Are Lost

God has a strong desire that men and women be saved, that no one would die without Christ. Paul told Timothy that God "wants all people to be saved and to come to a knowledge of the truth" (1 Tim. 2:4). We should have the same desire and therefore want to share the gospel with the lost. James said, "My brothers and sisters, if one of you should wander from the truth and someone should bring that person back, remember this: Whoever turns a sinner from the error of their way will save them from death and cover over a multitude of sins" (5:19–20). If, for example, we discovered some new technology or medical breakthrough, we would certainly want to share that information with the world. But our fear of being rejected or embarrassed keeps us from talking to people about Jesus Christ. We fear people more than God. God has certain expectations of us as His disciples. For example, God isn't going to speak to you in a small voice every time He wants us to love our neighbor. He has already commanded us to do that in Scriptures.

The command in Mark 16:15—"He said to them, 'Go into all the world and preach the gospel to all creation'"— requires some thought. What is the gospel anyway? The word *gospel* means "good news," so the gospel of Christ is the good news of His coming to provide forgiveness of sins for all who will believe. "Now, brothers and sisters, I want to remind you of the gospel I preached to you, which you received and on which you have taken your stand. By this gospel you are saved, if you hold firmly to the word I preached to you. Otherwise, you have believed in vain. For what I received I passed on to you as of first importance: that Christ died for our sins according to the Scriptures, that he was buried, that he was raised on the third day according to the Scriptures" (1 Cor. 15:1–4). There you have it, the biblical gospel, or good news, is the death, burial, and resurrection of the Lord Jesus Christ! What a person does with this news will determine where he or she spends eternity. God is calling you to choose life.

When we consider the enormity of the task of taking the gospel to the whole world, who could be adequate for such a mission? We are certainly not adequate of ourselves. How can we accomplish anything alone? Our adequacy comes from God! Without Him we can do nothing (John 15:4-6). Throughout Biblical history, God has worked through individuals to accomplish His purpose. Noah, Joseph, Moses, Joshua, David, Elijah, Elisha, (so many others) come to mind on how each served God. The Bible tells us that David served the purpose of God in his own generation. God is at work in all Christians. Paul told the church at Philippi, "being confident of this, that he who began a good work in you will carry it on to completion until the day of Christ Jesus." (Phil. 1:6). Again, Paul said, "for it is God who works in you to will and to act in order to fulfill his good purpose" (Phil. 2:13). We should not doubt that God works in and through us to accomplish His good purpose.

But how can we who have jobs and families just leave home and go all over the world? Not everyone can go into the world or even beyond their local city. Paul said, "And how can anyone preach unless they are sent?" (Rom. 10:15). Remember that in Mark 16:15 Christ was speaking to the eleven apostles just before His ascension. At that point it was up to them to start the mission work. Was it possible for them to accomplish this in their lifetime? Probably not. It has been estimated that

How Do We Walk in God's Path with Self-Assurance?

300 million people were alive at the time of Jesus' crucifixion and about 45 million of those people, including Jesus, lived in the Roman Empire.[1] Therefore, someone would have to continue the work after the disciples. The New Testament has many scriptures that assign this responsibility to all of Christ's disciples then and now. For example, "He commanded us to preach to the people and to testify that he is the one whom God appointed as judge of the living and the dead" (Acts 10:42) and "But you will receive power when the Holy Spirit comes on you; and you will be my witnesses in Jerusalem, and in all Judea and Samaria, and to the ends of the earth" (Acts 1:8).

Today there are Christians virtually all over the world, and if we all tell the good news to our neighbors, friends, and family in a combined effort, theoretically we could spread the message all over the world. But we must ask ourselves, are we doing our part to make it happen? Thankfully we have missionaries who can go and preach the gospel, and I believe it is our obligation to support our missionaries as much as we can. Don't forget how important prayer is in carrying out this commandment. We should pray for our missionaries and ourselves in spreading the gospel.

A study conducted by LifeWay Research found 80 percent of those who attend church one or more times a month, believe they have a personal responsibility to share their faith, but 61 percent had not told another person about how to become a Christian in the previous six months. Are we ashamed of the gospel?[2] Are we embarrassed about our faith in Christ? We are to fear God more than people! (Matt. 10:28) A stern warning comes from Christ: "I tell you, whoever publicly acknowledges me before others, the Son of Man will also acknowledge before the angels of God. But whoever disowns me before others will be disowned before the angels of God" (Luke 12:8–9). Every soul is of *infinite* value to God. He was willing to

---

[1] Patrick J. Kiger, "The World of Ancient Judea: Life in the Land and Times of Jesus Christ," National Geographic, February 10, 2015, http://channel.nationalgeographic.com/killing-jesus/articles/history-of-jesus-era/.

[2] Romans 1:16

pay His own Son's life for it. Once we understand that, it should keep us ready to share the Gospel with every lost soul we meet. It is because a Christian has assurance of their own salvation that they can witness to others effectively.

I have a friend who hands out a printed card with a scripture and a short inspirational message whenever she talks to a stranger or gives someone a tip. I believe this is a good idea and an example of thinking outside the box. We may dismiss it, assuming that 99 percent of those go right into the trash. But even if just one person responds to it, how great would that be? Bottom line, every member of the Lord's church is important in spreading the gospel of Christ. "The things you have heard me say in the presence of many witnesses entrust to reliable people who will also be qualified to teach others" (2 Tim. 2:2). Faithful Christians honestly try to win others to Christ.

Glorifying God

First Corinthians 6:19–20 asks, "Do you not know that your bodies are temples of the Holy Spirit, who is in you, whom you have received from God? You are not your own; you were bought at a price. Therefore honor God with your bodies." To glorify God means we bring Him honor through what we say and how we act. To glorify God means to acknowledge His glory and to value it above all things. It means demonstrating our heartfelt gratitude. We glorify God through our faith, through our love, through our good deeds and through our desire to obey Him.

When we take credit for something we benefited from, we rob God of His due glory. When we give God all the glory, we are truly appreciating God and Jesus Christ, who alone deserve all the credit. But we can also bring shame to the name of Christ (and ourselves), if we claim to be a believer and do not live up to our claim.

Paul understood that what we do either glorifies God or glorifies ourselves and brings shame to His holy name. Paul said that "whether you eat or drink or whatever you do, do it all for the glory of God" (1 Cor. 10:31). We should glorify God in our words, in our actions, and in our service to Jesus Christ. "Whatever you do, work at it with all your heart, as working for the Lord, not for human masters, since you know that you will receive an inheritance from the Lord as a reward. It is the Lord Christ you are serving" (Col. 3:23–24).

The New Testament abounds with statements that assert the importance of works in relation to Christian assurance. Heaven is a prepared place for a prepared people. In the Sermon on the Mount, Christ said, "Let your light shine before others, that they may see your good deeds and glorify your Father in heaven" (Matt. 5:16).

Loving God Rather Than Loving the World

We are told not to love the things of the world, because if we do, the love of God is not in us (1 John 2:15). The things of the world include family. Jesus plainly tells us that "anyone who loves their father or mother more than me is not worthy of me; anyone who loves their son or daughter more than me is not worthy of me" (Matt. 10:37). James said, "Don't you know that friendship with the world means enmity against God? Therefore, anyone who chooses to be a friend of the world becomes an enemy of God" (James 4:4). Most Christians spend more time on the computer, watching television, or working on their hobbies than they do reading the Bible or praying. By themselves, these secular activities are not wrong, but when we spend an inordinate amount of time on them, we are showing God that they are our real priorities. How we spend our time shows us where our hearts are.

Matthew 6:19–24 records Jesus' statement that we tend to store up personal possessions, including money:

> Do not store up for yourselves treasures on earth, where moths and vermin destroy, and where thieves break in and steal. But store up for yourselves treasures in heaven, where moths and

vermin do not destroy, and where thieves do not break in and steal. For where your treasure is, there your heart will be also...

No one can serve two masters. Either you will hate the one and love the other, or you will be devoted to the one and despise the other. You cannot serve both God and money.

Our true priority should be seeking Christ and His kingdom, primarily because if we do, we will have all that we need.

Visiting Widows and Orphans

Visiting widows and orphans might be one of the most overlooked commandments in the New Testament, James describes it as pure and undefiled religion: "Religion that God our Father accepts as pure and faultless is this: to look after orphans and widows in their distress and to keep oneself from being polluted by the world" (James 1:27). We may to some extent care for the widows and orphans in our churches, but do we visit the nursing homes, where almost everyone is a widow and orphan? According to Bartlesville Examiner-Enterprise statistics prove 60 percent of the residents in nursing homes never have visitors. There are also great needs in children's homes and foster care. They need donations (monetary and other), both big and small, and perhaps even more important they need volunteers to donate their time.

Having Thankful Hearts

As Christians we can be genuinely happy, because we're right with God through faith in Jesus Christ, and we know that God is working all things together for good for those who love Him (Rom. 8:28–31). Paul directs us to give thanks in everything (Eph. 5:20; 1 Thess. 5:18) and to overflow with gratitude to God because of His great salvation that is so freely given (Col. 1:12; 2:6–7). We should always remember that everything we have is

How Do We Walk in God's Path with Self-Assurance?

a gift from God, and without gratefulness we become arrogant and self-centered. How do you think God feels when He's done so much for us and we are just "too busy" to thank Him for all our gifts? Do you think He can't wait to send us more blessings?

What we think about the most, directs our day. If we think about work all the time, we can become workaholics. If we think about video games all the time, you know what happens. If we dwell on our problems and negative things, we become pessimistic and ungrateful, and it can pull us down. One of the vital steps to developing a thankful heart is to meditate on the blessings that we have in our lives and the One they came from. Philippians 4:8 tells us what we should set our minds on: things that are true, noble, right, pure, lovely, admirable, excellent, and praiseworthy! First Thessalonians 5:16–18 states: "Rejoice always, pray continually, give thanks in all circumstances; for this is God's will for you in Christ Jesus."

Developing the Gifts of the Spirit

Spiritual gifts are empowerments given by the Holy Spirit to the followers of Christ so they can build up the body of Christ—the church—and extend the kingdom of God throughout the world. The spiritual gifts listed in 1 Corinthians 12:8–10 are wisdom, knowledge, faith, healing, miracles, prophecy, discerning of spirits, speaking in tongues, and interpretation of tongues. Similar lists appear in Ephesians 4:7–13 and Romans 12:3–8. The Holy Spirit is the dispenser of the spiritual gifts as He sees fit (1 Cor. 12:7, 11). As believers, we are stewards of the gifts of God (1 Peter 4:10). Second Peter 1:3 tells us that "His divine power has given us everything we need for a godly life through our knowledge of him who called us by his own glory and goodness." The gifts of the Holy Spirit are part of *everything we need* to fulfill His purposes for our lives. Many who claim to be Christians do not produce these fruits effectively. It takes more than saying we are Christians; it takes the Holy Spirit to produce the fruit of the Spirit in us. We produce fruit by our obedience to the Lord and by serving others in the cause of Christ. God does not give us spiritual gifts for our own benefit but for the benefit of others. God uses our words and actions to exhort, comfort, and edify those around us.

Finding Our Gifts

The Holy Spirit distributes His gifts as He sees fit (1 Cor. 12:7–11). God does not want us to be ignorant of how He wants us to serve Him. The first and most obvious thing we learn from this text is that spiritual gifts are for *strengthening* others. If someone's faith is in jeopardy, we should think about how we can help that person. Then we do or say what seems most helpful, and if the person is helped, we may have discovered one of our gifts. There is no magic formula or spiritual-gift test to tell us what gifts of the Spirit we possess. We just need to focus on serving God by studying the scriptures regarding spiritual gifts, pray and look for ways to help. Do you see a need in your church, community, or family? Do what you can do. If we seek God's will and obey His teaching, He will equip us with the gifts of the Spirit we need.

Using Our Gifts

The apostle Paul indicated that the gifts of the Spirit are equally valid but not equally valuable (1 Cor. 12:31). Their value is determined by their worth to the church. To explain this, he used the analogy of the human body. All members of the body have different functions, Paul declared, but some are more important than others (1 Cor. 12:12–26). The service of each Christian should be in proportion to the gifts that person possesses. All believers, as members of the body of Christ, must serve in order for the body to be fully functional. That is why a church needs pastors, teachers, helpers, servants, administrators, and people with great faith. All the gifts of the Holy Spirit need to work together to reach the full potential of the church. Since the gifts of the Spirit are gifts of grace, their use must be controlled by love, the greatest of all the gifts of the Spirit (1 Cor. 13).

God has given us spiritual gifts for many purposes. Ultimately, they have been provided to equip us to glorify God. The gifts of the Spirit were given "to equip his people for works of service, so that the body of Christ may be built up until we all reach unity in the faith and in the knowledge of the Son of God and become mature, attaining to the whole measure of the fullness of Christ.... Instead, speaking the truth in love, we will grow to become in every respect the mature body of him who is the head, that is, Christ" (Eph. 4:12–13, 15).

Jesus is our perfect example; He exemplified all the spiritual gifts through the words He spoke and the actions He carried out. Since Jesus is now at the right hand of God the Father, the Holy Spirit is the primary manifestation of the presence of God on the earth. Our heavenly Father distributes the gifts of the Spirit among the members of His Body so believers can now glorify God through those gifts.

Live as Christians

When the book of Titus was written, the church in Crete was a new congregation. The focus of Paul's teaching to these new believers was how to begin living the Christian life so they could be an example of the grace of God to their pagan neighbors. The heart of Titus can be summed up in a twofold theme: to do good works for themselves, especially for the sake of outsiders. Paul instructed Titus to review with the Cretans the responsibilities Christians have toward those in authority and others in general, to consider how one is saved by God's mercy through the washing of regeneration and renewal of the Holy Spirit, and to maintain good works while avoiding things that are unprofitable and useless (including some individuals).

> Remind the people to be subject to rulers and authorities, to be obedient, to be ready to do whatever is good, to slander no one, to be peaceable and considerate, and always to be gentle toward everyone.
>
> At one time we too were foolish, disobedient, deceived and enslaved by all kinds of passions and pleasures. We lived in malice and envy, being hated and hating one another. But when the kindness and love of God our Savior appeared, he saved us, not because of righteous things we had done, but because of his mercy. He saved us through the washing of rebirth and renewal by the Holy Spirit, whom he poured out on us generously through Jesus Christ our Savior, so that, having been justified by his grace, we might become heirs having the hope of eternal life. This is a trustworthy saying. And I want you to stress these things, so that those who have trusted in God may be careful to devote themselves to doing what is good. These things are excellent and profitable for everyone.
>
> But avoid foolish controversies and genealogies and arguments and quarrels about the law, because these are unprofitable and useless. Warn a divisive person once, and then warn them a second time. After that, have nothing to do with them. You may be sure that such people are warped and sinful; they are self-condemned (Titus 3:1–11).

Conclusion

To summarize; faithfulness is a requirement for every Christian. We must be devoted and firmly hold to the teachings of the Bible, and live true to its commands. As God is faithful, He expects us to likewise be faithful. When Jesus says, "The one who endures to the end will be saved" (Matthew 24:13, ESV). He is speaking of those who are true followers of Jesus Christ, who will withstand the onslaught of wickedness, recognize and reject false teaching, and cling fast to the truth of God's Word. Doing right in God's sight is not always easy. Remember, God knows if we are faithful or not, and He will reward or punish us according to our life.

Those who stay faithful study the Bible regularly: "Study to show thyself approved unto God, a workman that needeth not to be ashamed, rightly dividing the word of truth" (2 Timothy 2:15). The Bible reveals God's will to us so that we may worship and serve God acceptably.

Those who stay faithful pray regularly: "Then He spoke a parable to them, that men always ought to pray and not lose heart" (Luke 18:1). God's people must be praying people. Christians have not done the best they can until they pray.

Those who stay faithful attend all the services of the church: Hebrews 10:25 is a warning to Christians. "Not forsaking the assembling of ourselves together, as is the manner of some, but exhorting one another, and so much the more as you see the day approaching." Those who do not remain steadfast in worship become weak spiritually, sickly spiritually and even die spiritually.

Those who stay faithful honestly try to win others to Christ: The daily life of a Christian involves soul winning. "And daily in the temple, and in every house, they did not cease teaching and preaching Jesus as the Christ" (Acts 5:42). Every member of the Lord's church is important in the spreading of the gospel of Christ.

God's Word is the everlasting seed that makes possible one to be born again (1 Pet. 1:23; James 1:21). His gospel has the power to save (Rom. 1:16; 1 Cor. 1:21). His love and kindness move people to repentance (Rom. 2:4). We love, because He first loved us (1 John 4:19). We have a living hope, because Jesus rose from the dead (1 Pet. 1:3-5). We are able to produce fruit because He provides the seed for the sower (2 Cor. 9:8-10).

God's people are zealous for good works (Titus 2:14). The love Christians have for God shows in their Bible study, church attendance, prayer life, and evangelism. Are these four qualities, which keep people faithful, present in your life?

7

How Can We Be Open to God's Discipline as a Tool to Make Us Faithful Christians?

Discipline is often a touchy subject. I have never met anyone who said that discipline was pleasant. As kids most of us were disciplined by our parents as they tried to train us to be responsible adults. Now as adults we dread facing discipline in our lives, whether it's from our boss, a spiritual leader at church, or God, because it usually means we have to face the consequences of a bad decision we made. God's loving discipline of His children is one of the most practical truths in the Bible, and if we don't understand it, we won't persevere when trials hit, as they certainly will.

At the moment of salvation, the Holy Spirit comes to dwell in our spirit. God then begins the supernatural work of transforming us, His children, into the image of His Son, Jesus Christ, who was and is perfect (Rom. 8:29). As we mature in our faith, God uses tests and trials to develop our character and spiritual leadership. By responding to trials in the grace of God, we experience the power of God's Spirit, which will be manifested in our lives through the fruit of the Spirit: love, joy, peace, longsuffering, gentleness, goodness, faith, meekness, and self-control (Gal. 5:22–23). When God disciplines us, it is almost always because of sin in our hearts and lives. His discipline comes in different forms, but it always has the same purpose: that we would be trained by it so we may share in God's holiness with peace. The author of Hebrews wrote, "My son, do not make light of the Lord's discipline, and do not lose heart when he rebukes you, *because the Lord disciplines the one he loves*, and he chastens *everyone* he accepts as his son....

Endure hardship as discipline; God is treating you as his children. For what children are not disciplined by their father?" (Heb. 12:5–7)

We cannot truly love our children without there being some form of correction. As parents, we would never let our children play near a highway. Love motivates parents to discipline their children if they continue to put themselves in danger. God does the same. He says, "Those whom I love I rebuke and discipline. So be earnest and repent" (Rev. 3:19). The Israelites disobeyed the Lord and served other gods. So God sent them into captivity to humble them and bring them to repentance. Through this discipline the Jewish nation learned to worship only God (at least temporarily). Likewise, God may punish us for our sins, but it is always a call to repent and return to Him. Why? Because He loves us!

This passage gives a very human illustration: "They [our fathers] disciplined us for a little while as they thought best; but God disciplines us for our good, in order that we may share in his holiness" (Heb. 12:10). The point? No discipline is pleasant at the time but instead is painful. However, later it produces righteousness and peace for those who have been trained by it.

I grew up in a strict home where ample discipline was handed out to my brothers and me, but our parents always helped us understand why we were being punished. Like the time I set the back porch on fire at age seven. We lived in the country, and my mother burned the trash outside in a barrel. One day I decided to help her out and burn the trash for her. Because it was cold outside, I thought it would be more convenient to burn it on the back porch. It's obvious what happened, the whole back porch caught on fire. After my mother put the fire out, she promptly set my pants on fire. But then she explained how serious the consequences of my actions could have been—that I could have burned down the house and we wouldn't have had a place to live. I responded, "Why don't you spank me again?" I was grief-stricken, and I never played with matches again. So, the discipline was effective, as God wants His discipline of Christians to be.

How Can We Be Open to God's Discipline as a Tool to Make Us Faithful Christians?

Here's the point: if we step back and analyze the discipline God gives us, we will be able to understand that God wants to keep us in a loving and obedient relationship with Him so we may live with Him in the place He has already prepared for us in heaven. The Scriptures say that discipline from God is evidence of His love. When we consistently discipline a child and do it with the right attitude and are focused on the child's best interests, we are expressing love exactly as God expresses His love to Christians. God told the Hebrew Christians that the adversity they faced came from His loving hand, not necessarily because they were bad, but because He wanted the best for them (Heb. 12:5–6). That's His motivation with us as well.

How Does God's Discipline Differ from Punishment?

According to the Bible, God's grace saves Christians from the punishment we deserve, but it does not always save us from the consequences of our actions and it never saves us from God's discipline. God's punishment stems from His *wrath* against sin, but His discipline stems from His *love* for His children. Punishment is God acting as Judge; discipline is God acting as Father. Under punishment, the sinner pays for his sins. Under discipline, Christ has already paid for our sins. Sometimes God's discipline is directly related to a specific sin in His children, at other times it is an opportunity to develop growth and maturity. Just as God designed the human body to heal a broken bone, so has He equipped the body of Christ with all that is necessary to be involved in the process of restoring broken parts damaged by sin. "Endure hardship as discipline; God is treating you as his children. For what children are not disciplined by their father? If you are not disciplined—and everyone undergoes discipline—then you are not legitimate, not true sons and daughters at all" (Heb. 12:7-8).

Consider self-discipline—examining ourselves—as a proactive measure we can take in our lives. Self-discipline enables us to make the correct choices in our lives, which will lead to positive results. Exercising self-discipline is the key to ensuring we will experience the next level in our lives that God wants for us. If we are faithful in little things, we will be faithful in the big things (Luke 16:10).

If we blow off discipline without seeing God's loving hand in it, we are regarding it lightly. Can we assume that minor frustrations, like being late for an appointment because the traffic was worse than usual, as discipline? Rather than fuming at a traffic jam, can we see it as God lovingly giving us an opportunity to develop patience? To grow in godliness, should we treat *every* trial as God's loving discipline, specifically tailored to us as an opportunity to grow closer and be more obedient to Him? Hebrews 12: 7–11 warns us not to regard these trials lightly but to have humble, submissive attitudes and desire to bear the peaceful fruit of righteousness as we are conformed to the image of Christ. The discipline of enduring trials and sufferings ends up attesting that we are God's children.

I realize that it is difficult to understand how God can allow the terrible suffering that we see in the world. Many have gone so far as to allow painful sufferings to turn them away from God. But to cease to believe in God because of sorrow does not make God cease to exist, nor does it resolve the problem. Trials are a fact of life, but how we respond to them is our choice

Until a few years ago I had not considered the difficulties that were happening to me as disciplinary acts by God. Sometimes we are unaware of our sins or shortcomings until God brings some trial that exposes them. Affliction can make us aware of sins that we have not seen before. I have come to the realization that I missed several opportunities in my life to recognize I was being disciplined, opportunities to discover and stop committing those sins that I might grow closer to God. Perhaps the greatest reason God has for taking us through the trials of life is to bring us to the conclusion that we need Him. If we resist and harden our hearts, we will miss the purpose of the discipline. For example, I occasionally spent beyond my means on frivolous stuff, money wasted that could have been given to

How Can We Be Open to God's Discipline as a Tool to Make Us Faithful Christians?

church or the needy. I noticed that when my overspending occurred, unexpected expenses—home repairs, car repairs—would *always* occur. One such time I didn't have enough money to make my normal contribution to church on Sunday morning, and I thought, *I get paid next week, and I will double up then. It's no big deal.* In the next few days my air conditioner broke and my washing machine had to be replaced. I thought, *God, You now have my attention!* I examined myself for wrong doing and realized that in addition to my overspending, I had been shirking some of my Christian responsibilities; not attending some of the church services and not reading the Bible and praying regularly. Simply put, I had been neglecting my relationship with God. I viewed this as God training me to use wisely the things He has blessed me with. I prayed for forgiveness and moved forward to a better relationship with God. Our response to God's discipline must be trusting Him as our loving, sovereign heavenly Father. To endure the struggle against evil, whether the trial is big or little, we must submit to Him in faith, viewing His discipline as a sign of His love.

How Do We Know If We're Being Disciplined?

The Lord's discipline is an often-ignored fact of life for believers. We often complain about our circumstances without realizing that they could be the consequences of our very own sin and are a part of the Lord's loving discipline because of that sin. Discipline is not to be confused with cold-hearted punishment. The Lord's discipline is a response of His love for us and His desire for each of us to be holy. God will use testing, trials, and various predicaments to bring us back to Him in repentance. The result of His discipline is a stronger faith and a renewed relationship with God (James 1:2-4), not to mention destroying the hold that particular sin had over us.

Based on the scriptures we've read, I believe all Christians are disciplined by God. The Lord's discipline works for our own good, that He might be glorified in our lives.

Is it Possible to Know We Are Saved?

Because Christians have trusted in the sacrifice of Christ on the cross, they are exempt from the *eternal* punishment of God, which is damnation, or the casting of the person into hell forever (Matt. 8:12; 25:30; Rev. 14:9–11). This kind of punishment will never happen to those who have faith and believe in the atoning sacrifice of Jesus. The reason God disciplines Christians is that He loves us and wants us to improve our relationship with Him (Heb.12:6; 9-16) and with others (Matt. 22:39). When we sin, we hinder our fellowship with God (Isa. 59:2), and since God desires fellowship with us (1 Cor. 1:9), He must lovingly discipline the Christian who is not walking properly before Him.

The Bible has a lot to say about the importance of disciplining children. Proverbs 19:18 states it boldly: "Discipline your children, for in that there is hope; do not be a willing party to their death." Children who experience little or no discipline often grow up to be stubborn, unmanageable, misguided, rebellious teenagers and adults. The same applies to God's discipline of us. When troubles set in and trials arrive, a lot of us wonder, *Am I really saved? If I were really saved, why would I be having all these problems? Has God forsaken me? I'm a Christian; I'm not supposed to have so many problems. If God really loved me, He wouldn't let these things happen to me.* Certainly He would! According to the Scriptures, discipline proves that He loves us.

Think about this: God does not discipline *unsaved* people in this life, because they are not His children. He saves their judgment for the Great White Throne Judgment, when their sins will be exposed, and all who are not His children will be cast into the lake of fire. Unsaved people are Satan's children, and he wreaks havoc on them.

Paul handled his discipline in a positive manner, as he stated in 2 Corinthians 12:7: "In order to keep me from becoming conceited, I was given a thorn in my flesh, a messenger of Satan, to torment me."

Here are some additional scriptures to consider regarding discipline:

How Can We Be Open to God's Discipline as a Tool to Make Us Faithful Christians?

Hebrews 12:5–11:
My son do not make light of the Lord's discipline, and do not lose heart when he rebukes you, because the Lord disciplines the one he loves, and he chastens everyone he accepts as his son.

Endure hardship as discipline; God is treating you as his children. For what children are not disciplined by their father? If you are not disciplined—and everyone undergoes discipline—then you are not legitimate, not true sons and daughters at all. Moreover, we have all had human fathers who disciplined us, and we respected them for it. How much more should we submit to the Father of spirits and live! They disciplined us for a little while as they thought best; but God disciplines us for our good, in order that we may share in his holiness. No discipline seems pleasant at the time, but painful. Later, however, it produces a harvest of righteousness and peace for those who have been trained by it.

First Peter 4:12–16:
Dear friends do not be surprised at the fiery ordeal that has come on you to test you, as though something strange were happening to you. But rejoice inasmuch as you participate in the sufferings of Christ, so that you may be overjoyed when his glory is revealed. If you are insulted because of the name of Christ, you are blessed, for the Spirit of glory and of God rests on you. If you suffer, it should not be as a murderer or thief or any other kind of criminal, or even as a meddler. However, if you suffer as a Christian, do not be ashamed, but praise God that you bear that name.

Is it Possible to Know We Are Saved?

James 1:2–6:
Consider it pure joy, my brothers and sisters, whenever you face trials of many kinds, because you know that the testing of your faith produces perseverance. Let perseverance finish its work so that you may be mature and complete, not lacking anything. If any of you lacks wisdom, you should ask God, who gives generously to all without finding fault, and it will be given to you. But when you ask, you must believe and not doubt, because the one who doubts is like a wave of the sea, blown and tossed by the wind.

John 9:1–5:
As he went along, he saw a man blind from birth. His disciples asked him, "Rabbi, who sinned, this man or his parents, that he was born blind?"

"Neither this man nor his parents sinned," said Jesus, "but this happened so that the works of God might be displayed in him. As long as it is day, we must do the works of him who sent me. Night is coming, when no one can work. While I am in the world, I am the light of the world."

Notice the disciples thought that sin was the cause of this man's malformation, but Jesus informed them that was not true in this case but rather an opportunity that God might be displayed when Jesus healed him.

Were Ananias and Sapphira punished or disciplined by God?

In the early Christian church in Jerusalem, the believers sold their excess land or possessions and donated the money, so no one would go hungry. Ananias and his wife Sapphira, members of the church, sold a piece of property but kept back part of the proceeds for themselves and gave the rest to the church. Just to be clear, there was no necessity upon any of the

How Can We Be Open to God's Discipline as a Tool to Make Us Faithful Christians?

people of the church in Jerusalem to give to the Lord anything of their possessions. There was no condemnation upon those who did not sell their property to meet the needs of the poor and unfortunate.

The Apostle Peter, questioned their honesty and said: "Ananias, how is it that Satan has so filled your heart that you have lied to the Holy Spirit and have kept for yourself some of the money you received for the land? What made you think of doing such a thing? You have not lied to men but to God" (Acts 5:3-4). Ananias, on hearing this, immediately fell down dead. Three hours later, Ananias' wife Sapphira came in, not knowing what had happened.

Peter asked her if the amount they donated was the full price of the land. "Yes, that is the price," she lied. Peter said to her, "How could you agree to test the Spirit of the Lord?" (Acts 5:9). Just like her husband, she instantly fell down dead. With this show of God's anger, great fear seized everyone in the young church. The sin which Ananias and Sapphira committed was that of lying and hypocrisy. God dealt in severe discipline upon Ananias and Sapphira to show the church that it is imperative that hypocrisy and impurity not be allowed in His church.

The Bible does not tell us who caused their deaths (though it seems rather obvious), but as Christians we must understand that Satan seeks to influence our lives. By refusing to yield to a sinful lifestyle, we prevent Satan from having the influence over us that he desires. Had Ananias and Sapphira not succumbed to the temptation of misrepresenting their level of generosity, Satan would have had no influence over them, and this tragic episode could have been avoided. It is amazing to discover the things we can learn about God's character and how He works in our lives and churches from this short and sometimes overlooked story of Ananias and Sapphira.

According to the Bible, God's grace saves Christians from the punishment we deserve, but it does not always save us from the consequences of our actions and it never saves us from God's discipline. Consequences are often what we deal with in the present. Discipline looks towards a better future. Being disciplined gives you the strength to withstand hardships and difficulties, whether physical, emotional or mental.

Conclusion

God disciplines those whom he loves, and He gets our attention with trials and difficult circumstances. God's Word in Scripture serves as the mouthpiece, the voice in our ears to correct, console, rebuke, train, and so on. This is fatherly "discipline." Notice how close the word *discipline* is to another biblical word, *disciple*. God's discipline serves to help us grow as Christ's disciples. The trials we face are divinely designed to mature us so that we become more serviceable disciples in Christ's church and kingdom.

God's fatherly discipline is for believers only. No doubt, unbelievers can also learn a lot through the hard knocks of life, and as a result they might become a better person. But life's ace Jesus' disciples through suffering. God's discipline toward His children, however, is sanctifying. His discipline is love in action, for He loves us not by spoiling us but by correcting us and making us prosperous disciples.

In every trial, whether major or minor, stop and examine your heart. Are you truly in submission to God? Are you seeking to learn and grow in holiness through the trial? The lessons we learn from discipline help us to not make the same mistakes again: "God disciplines us for our good, that we may share in his holiness" (Hebrews 12:10). I think the person who asks, "How do I know if I am being disciplined?" might ask instead, "How do I know if I have sinned?" The answer to that is: Read your Bible.

8

How Can We Achieve Assurance?

Jesus Christ speaks of our ability to know that we are abiding in grace, which is important and must be taken seriously. Paul wrote at the end of his life, "I have fought the good fight, I have finished the race, I have kept the faith. Now there is in store for me the crown of righteousness, which the Lord, the righteous Judge, will award to me on that day—and not only to me, but also to all who have longed for his appearing" (2 Timothy 4:7–8).

The New Testament teaches us that genuine assurance is possible and desirable, but it also warns us that we can be deceived through a false assurance. Jesus declared, "Not everyone who says to me, 'Lord, Lord,' will enter the kingdom of heaven, but only the one who does the will of my Father who is in heaven" (Matt. 7:21). By examining our Christian lives, we can be *confident* of our present salvation and *confident* we have not thrown away that gift of grace. "As for you, see that what you have heard from the beginning remains in you. If it does, you also will remain in the Son and in the Father" (1 John 2:24). Jesus said, "Remain in me, as I also remain in you. No branch can bear fruit by itself; it must remain in the vine. Neither can you bear fruit unless you remain in me. I am the vine; you are the branches. If you remain in me and I in you, you will bear much fruit; apart from me you can do nothing. If you do not remain in me, you are like a branch that is thrown away and withers; such branches are picked up, thrown into the fire and burned" (John 15:4–6). Jesus places strong emphasis on continued spiritual life, and our relationship with Him is conditional on our abiding in Him. This means we have the power to forsake Him and be lost if we choose.

There is a series of examinations in 1 John that we can use to test ourselves and our faith. As we look at them, we know that no one will get a perfect score, but when we're genuinely born of God, we will grow as we deal with the temptations around us: the world, the flesh, and the Devil. We will make progress in gaining more victories and losing fewer battles as we grow stronger in Christ and in the power of abiding in the Word of God. We should use these test questions listed below and test ourselves often to make sure we are continuing in our progress and growing in Christ. One of the primary reasons the Apostle John wrote his first letter was so that believers might be assured of their eternal destination. In his letter he examines the evidence to eternal life in chapters two through five, but in chapter one, he gives realities that a Christian must live within, if we are to contend with sin in an effective way. I highly recommend reading the five chapters of 1 John. They are relatively short chapters, but they contain so much information about how we should live our Christian lives.

Do We Enjoy Fellowship with Christ and Other Christians?

One of our deepest human longings is for intimacy. We hope to find it in marriage. Perhaps we have found it with a friend or group of friends from church. We should certainly desire for an intimate relationship with God but we sometimes wonder if such closeness is actually possible. First John 1:3 says, "We proclaim to you what we have seen and heard, so that you also may have fellowship with us. And our fellowship is with the Father and with his Son, Jesus Christ." In the same way that we need to spend time with God in order to grow, we need to spend time with other Christians so that we are encouraged in our faith whether we are facing struggles or experiencing joys. Hebrews 10:24–25 tells us to assemble with other believers, and Romans 12:5 and 1 Corinthians 12:12-27 talk about how we all need each other to function properly. Have you experienced communion with God and Christ? Have you experienced the joy of talking to God? In John 13:35 Jesus says, "By this everyone will know that you are my disciples, if you love one another."

Do We Bear Much Fruit?

In John 15:5 Jesus said, "I am the vine; you are the branches. If you remain in me and I in you, you will bear much fruit; apart from me you can do nothing." In John 15:16 Jesus said, "You did not choose me, but I chose you and appointed you so that you might go and bear fruit—fruit that will last—and so that whatever you ask in my name the Father will give you." If we bear fruit, we love people and win people to Christ. Jesus explained how fruit bearing can be accomplished: if we abide in Him, He will abide in us. We must keep ourselves closely attached to the vine—Jesus. Everything we try to do will come to nothing unless we do it through Jesus Christ. It is the secret of all fruitfulness.

Do We Walk in Light or in Darkness?

John said, "If we claim to have fellowship with him and yet walk in the darkness, we lie and do not live out the truth. But if we walk in the light, as he is in the light, we have fellowship with one another, and the blood of Jesus, His Son, purifies us from all sin" (1 John 1:6–7). Walking in the light is directly related to following Jesus. Walking in the light means we consider Jesus as the light in this world, and we walk in that light by following His commandments, living in His power, and growing in His grace. Walking in darkness means living in sin or, simply put, being without God. "If we claim to be without sin, we deceive ourselves and the truth is not in us" (1 John 1:8). Light and darkness do not coexist.

Do We Admit and Confess Our Sins?

"If we claim to be without sin, we deceive ourselves and the truth is not in us" (1 John 1:8). Believers in Christ understand that they don't have to sin. But when (not if) they do, they know to go to Jesus Christ, the believer's advocate. That's a reassuring reality to hold on to when confronted with personal sin. "No one who lives in him keeps on sinning. No one who continues to sin has either seen him or known him. Dear children do not let anyone lead you astray. The one who does what is right is righteous, just as he is righteous. The one who does what is sinful is of the devil, because the devil has been sinning from the beginning. The reason the Son of God appeared was to destroy the devil's work. No one who is born of God will continue to sin, because God's seed remains in them; they cannot go on sinning, because they have been born of God" (1 John 3:6–9).

Do We Keep His Commandments?

"We know that we have come to know him if we keep his commandments. Whoever says, 'I know him,' but does not do what he commands is a liar, and the truth is not in that person. But if anyone obeys his word, love for God is truly made complete in them. This is how we know we are in him" (1 John 2:3–5). This couldn't be clearer: If we want to know whether we're true Christians, and that our love for God is true, we should ask ourselves *"do we obey the commandments of Christ?"* We see through the Scripture that when we obey, we demonstrate that we have a relationship with God, that He is our Father, and that we have genuine faith. We demonstrate that we have truly been born again into the family of God. We must live as God's obedient children. Admittedly, we have a part to play in our spiritual journey with Christ, but God has done the "heavy lifting." The part that remains for us is neither impossible nor beyond our grasp (1 Cor. 10:13). We see that our love for God must be accompanied by obedience to His will. We should strive not to slip back into our old ways of living to satisfy our own desires.

Do Our Lives Indicate We Love God Rather Than the World?

"Do not love the world or anything in the world. If anyone loves the world, love for the Father is not in them. For everything in the world—the lust of the flesh, the lust of the eyes, and the pride of life—comes not from the Father but from the world" (1 John 2:15–16).

As I sat in church one Sunday, I saw a little girl no more than four, looking at her father so sweetly as she reached and gave him the biggest hug. I thought how much she must love him and was so completely dependent on him and, likewise, how much he loved her and would protect her at all cost. It dawned on me that's how we should love God. We should love Him as little children love, because that is what we are. "See what great love the Father has lavished on us, that we should be called children of God! And that is what we are! The reason the world does not know us is that it did not know him" (1 John 3:1). "And he said: 'Truly I tell you, unless you change and become like little children, you will never enter the kingdom of heaven. Therefore, whoever takes the lowly position of this child is the greatest in the kingdom of heaven'" (Matt. 18:3–4).

What should we learn from children? What qualities do they possess, and what examples do they provide that can help us in our own spiritual development? God wants us to come before Him as children, because children are innocent and trust with pure, uncorrupted hearts. Children come to their loving parents, trusting them completely to take care of them, to protect them, to provide for them, and to love and cherish them. They exemplify humility, obedience, and love. They are often the first to love and the first to forgive.

Do you love God, His truth, His kingdom, and all that He stands for? "For the grace of God has appeared that offers salvation to all people. It teaches us to say 'No' to ungodliness and worldly passions, and to live self-controlled, upright and godly lives in this present age, while we wait for the blessed hope—the appearing of the glory of our great God and Savior, Jesus Christ, who gave himself for us to redeem us from all wickedness and to purify for himself a people that are his very own, eager to do what is good" (Titus 2:11–14).

Are Our Lives Characterized by Doing What Is Right?

"If you know that he is righteous, you know that everyone who does what is right has been born of him" (1 John 2:29). I have in my own family a notable story about doing what is right. When my father passed away, my son gave the eulogy at his funeral service, and he recalled going with Dad to a town twenty-five miles away to buy building supplies. Just before they got home, my dad gave him the receipt and the cash he had gotten back and told my son to keep the change, which should have been about two dollars. When my son looked at it, there was an additional five-dollar bill. He told my dad, and they turned around and drove all the way back to the store. My son asked, "Why now? We are almost home." My dad said, "The cashier might get in trouble, or the company might take it out of her check. We need to make it right today." Clearly it made a very positive impression on my son for him to remember it all these years.

Do We See a Decreasing Pattern of Sin in Our Lives?

"But you know that he appeared so that he might take away our sins. And in him is no sin. No one who lives in him keeps on sinning. No one who continues to sin has either seen him or known him" (1 John 3:5–6). We cannot achieve a total absence of sin, but this refers to not continuing in sin as a way of life. Sin makes us not only guilty but also unclean before a holy God. The blood-wrought cleansing enables us to be restored to fellowship with God as "a people that are his very own" (1 John 1:7; Titus 2:14). Since we have been redeemed by His blood, Christ desires that we voluntarily yield ourselves wholly to Him

How Can We Achieve Assurance?

(1 Peter 1:18–19). Such a surrender is mankind's only judicious response to divine mercy (Rom. 12:1–2). Christians sometimes doubt their salvation because they can't seem to break sinful habits. John is not saying that the frequent occurrence of sin in a person's life means that person is lost. Rather, he clarifies his meaning by saying that a true believer cannot practice lawlessness—living as if there were no laws (1 John 3:4–6).

Do We Love Other Christians?

"We know that we have passed from death to life, because we love each other. Anyone who does not love remains in death" (John 3:14). Do you routinely love other believers? If we claim to be Christians but have no love in our hearts for those in the church or any track record of meeting their needs, then the apostle John says we're in the dark in spite of our claims to be in the light. John defined love as making sacrifices for others. The assurance that we are Christians, that our faith is the real thing, will come by the way we love. We should examine whether we love other Christians as evidenced by our deeds of kindness and sacrifice.

Do We Maintain a Clear Conscience?

"Dear friends, if our hearts do not condemn us, we have confidence before God" (1 John 3:21). To maintain a clear conscience that is sensitive to the Spirit of God, we must confess every sin we are conscious of and walk in the light of God's Word. The Holy Spirit always uses God's Word to reveal sin to us, and the blood of Jesus cleanses us of all sin. Scripture tells us to "keep hold of the deep truths of the faith with a clear conscience" (1 Tim. 3:9).

Do We Demonstrate Our Salvation to Others?

The apostle John gave all these tests to provide the true believer a biblical basis for confidence. If we can truthfully answer yes to these questions (or at least many of them and are working on the others) then our lives are bearing the fruit of true salvation. Jesus said that by our fruits we are known as His disciples (Matt. 7:20). Genuine saving faith will always produce works; a faith that continues without works is no faith at all and saves no one. We must cling to Christ and test ourselves, or prove to ourselves that we are in alignment with God's mind and will, and to make certain we continue to bring honor to God and Christ.

The evidence of salvation by good works does not mean that every believer will grow at the same rate or bear the same fruit. Matthew says, "But the seed falling on good soil refers to someone who hears the word and understands it. This is the one who produces a crop, yielding a hundred, sixty or thirty times what was sown" (13:23). We all have different talents and gifts. Luke says in Luke 12:48, "But the one who does not know and does things deserving punishment will be beaten with few blows. From everyone who has been given much, much will be demanded; and from the one who has been entrusted with much, much more will be asked." God gives us resources such as time and money to allow us to demonstrate our faith in action. We can show this by becoming a friend to someone who is lonely, gladly doing volunteer work, teaching, and encouraging others. We should ask God for wisdom on how to use these resources and commit ourselves to disbursing them according to His will so that He may be glorified.

Should We Make Plans for Our Christian Life?

Don't you wish that God had laid out a specific plan for the Christian life? Well, He did! But we need to come back to this simple formula if we want to remain Christians and generate renewal in the church. The formula? Keep God's commands in the New Testament. This is so important. Actually, our eternal life depends on it.

We should not leave our work for Christ to chance. Consider making a plan for doing God's will and keeping His commandments. God made a plan for our salvation before the beginning of time: to send Christ to earth to die for our sins. Is that not the greatest example we could have? Thousands of years were spent laying the groundwork to fulfill this plan. Also, Paul made plans to share the good news (2 Cor. 1:16; Acts 15:36; Rom. 1:13), the apostles made plans (Acts 6:1–3), and even Jesus Himself made plans during his life to fulfill his ministry on earth. (Matt 10:5–15; 16:21; 26:17–19).

In our daily living we plan our days around sporting events, family events, and other commitments. We use calendars and lists as ways to remind us of the things we want and need to do. Clearly, we think they are important enough to keep up with. Isn't that the least we could do for God? Our daily events pale in comparison to the things God has asked us to do. For example, make a list of His commandments, use a Christian planner or whatever works for you, and create a weekly, if not daily, schedule of the things you want to accomplish. Set your routine, study the Bible, pray for opportunities to do his work, and then you can make sure you are obeying His word. Our work for God is too important to leave it to chance. On Saturdays when I do my "big" house cleaning, if I don't make a list and stay focused, at the end of the day half of the things I wanted to do haven't been done. So, doesn't it make sense to plan our work for God with the same diligence?

A while back I planned to visit my new neighbors and invite them to church, but it took me four or five weeks to finally get around to it. If I had put it on my calendar (which I am now using), it would have been done right away. (By the way she visited the next Sunday). Schedule a time to write cards to send to the sick or bereaved from your church. Our daily prayer is so important, and we should add others from church or work to our lists.

Our good use of time can make all the difference in the world. Take time to pray, time to study, time to be with other Christians, and time to do good works. Never underestimate the value of redeeming your time (Eph. 5:15–16). We should set goals, but we must do so in humility, recognizing that God alone controls our destiny. We ought not to be so anxious about life that we make rigid plans that are beyond our capacity to keep, nor should we be so careless as to make no plans at all. It is wise to make plans for our lives, but when we talk about the future, let us remember to say, "If the Lord wills" (James 4:13–15). Let us be concerned about doing the Lord's will *today* and not worry about tomorrow. We could become discouraged if we think years into the future. Jesus said, "Therefore do not worry about tomorrow, for tomorrow will worry about itself. Each day has enough trouble of its own" (Matt. 6:34). Let us work for Jesus and do His will today. Let us ask God to help us be faithful today, and if tomorrow comes, we can continue with our plan.

Are We Ready to Stand Before God on Judgement Day?

Jesus says the road that leads to life is narrow and difficult. God hasn't hidden anything from us. He has told us what we need to do. Because He rescued us from eternal damnation, we should never resent any of His requirements, even if they cost us our friends, family, possessions, or our lives (Luke 14:26). We must study His Word and grow closer to Him every day. When Christians faithfully keep His teachings, they will be worthy and hear, "Well done, good and faithful servant!" (Matt. 25:21). Is the reward—a home in heaven for all of eternity with God—worth the effort? Absolutely!

Based on the Scriptures, our sin is not greater than Christ's grace. Now, as always, our only hope is Jesus Christ. We do not have to doubt, guess, or wonder whether we are saved. God has made it possible for us to know that we are in a saved relationship with Him. Our salvation is not based upon our feelings, good works, or moral goodness but entirely on the Word of God.

We will learn what Christ wants us to do as we study and obey His Word. Our Bible knowledge will increase our desire to please Christ as we follow His commands. The desire we have to do His will is a confirmation that we belong to Him. Create opportunities to tell others about Christ, like my friend who talks to people in the Walmart checkout line. Let's face it. We are so busy with our daily lives that it is easy to put off our Christian responsibilities.

We need to remember that God is not looking for an opportunity to pluck us out of His fold. However, we must persevere in God's truth with gratitude and be convicted of our sins. Even in times of trial we need to acknowledge God's goodness and thank Him for His many blessings. Also, we do not need to live in fear that one day we will slip and "lose" God's gift. The New Testament teaches us that we will not achieve sinless perfection until we are glorified with Christ in the next life. When fear builds in your heart, resist the Devil. Instead, focus your attention on God, and thank Him for His limitless love that reaches out to us. Each of us is responsible to work out the implications of our salvation each day. We must rely on the Holy Spirit and His power, not on our own. But, yes, we must work.

From the scriptures I have presented in this study, four key points stand out as measures to test our assurance of salvation.

Do We Feel Convicted When We Sin?

Do we at times have an overwhelming sense that we did something wrong? We are convicted when we become mindful of how much our sin dishonors God or when we recognize the loathsomeness of our sin. The Holy Spirit not only convicts people of sin, but He also brings them to repentance (John 16:7-11). The Holy Spirit brings to light our relationship to God. The convicting power of the Holy Spirit opens our eyes to our sin and opens our hearts to receive His grace. If we continually sin without remorse, we should objectively examine our Christian lives.

Does the Truth Remain in Us?

"As for you, see that what you have heard from the beginning remains in you. If it does, you also will remain in the Son and in the Father. And this is what he promised us—eternal life" (1 John 2:24–25). Scripture teaches that one's final salvation depends on the state of the soul at death. As Jesus Himself said, "The one who stands firm to the end will be saved" (Matt. 24:13; 25:31–46). Because God is the supreme authority, we must obey Him. Jesus told His followers, "If you love me, keep my commands" (John 14:15). He also directed us, saying, "Therefore go and make disciples of all nations, baptizing them in the name of the Father and of the Son and of the Holy Spirit, and teaching them to obey everything I have commanded you. And surely, I am with you always, to the very end of the age" (Matt. 28:19–20).

Do We Pray and Study the Bible Daily?

This sounds so basic, but daily prayer and Bible study are powerful sources of help. The Scriptures tell us in Proverbs 30 that every word of God is flawless. For this reason, the Lord asks us to hear his words and to allow them to make us new. Part of the Christian life is diligent reading and study of the Word, accompanied by prayer for understanding and wisdom to have a closer relationship with God through the Holy Spirit. Our communication with God plays a big part in keeping us where we need to be spiritually. "Faith comes from hearing the message, and the message is heard through the word about Christ" (Rom. 10:17). Studying the Bible helps us grow in faith and "grow in the grace and knowledge of our Lord and Savior Jesus Christ. To him be glory both now and forever! Amen" (2 Peter 3:18). Peter said to "make every effort to add to your faith...knowledge.... For if you do these things, you will never stumble, and you will receive a rich welcome into the eternal kingdom of our Lord and Savior Jesus Christ" (2 Peter 1:5, 10–11). No wonder the Bible places so much emphasis on growing in the knowledge of God's will. The phrase "make every effort" pretty well says it all, doesn't it? That's how important biblical knowledge is. Plainly, our continual growth in correct Bible knowledge is essential to our future. Remember, "Blessed are those who hunger and thirst for righteousness, for they will be filled" (Matt. 5:6).

Do We Keep Christ's Commandments?

Keeping the commandments of God is not only a way to show our sincere love for Christ our Savior, but the Way to Eternal Life and the Kingdom of God. When asked by a young ruler about how to obtain eternal life, Jesus gave a simple and straight answer, "if you wish to enter into life, keep the commandments" (Matthew 19: 17). Hebrews 5:9 says Jesus became the author of eternal salvation for all who obey Him. Consider how Jesus said that we can *remain* in His love: "If you keep my commands, you will remain in my love, just as I have kept my Father's commands and remain in his love" (John 15:10). Keeping Christ's commands is essential for us to receive eternal salvation. Everything we need to do as Christians is in the commandments. "Blessed are they that do his commandments, that they may have right to the tree of life and may enter in through the gates into the city" (Rev. 22:14 KJV).

Will the Christian Life Be Easy?

It is easy to fall into sin but very painful to get out. It was easy for Adam and Eve to fall into sin, and we see how dangerous that was. The entire human race was affected, and our Lord had to deliver us from that sin by leaving His throne in heaven, coming down to this wicked world, living among the poor, and ultimately dying for us, and caused Him great agony. Even His sweat turned into blood. It caused Him dishonor as people spit at Him, ridiculed Him, beat Him and pulled His beard, as Isaiah prophesied in Isaiah 50:6–7. He was treated like a criminal, and it cost Him His life.

The Bible does not tell us it will be easy; in fact, it says just the opposite. Paul told the Philippians, "Therefore, my dear friends, as you have always obeyed—not only in my presence, but now much more in my absence—continue to work out your salvation with fear and trembling, for it is God who works in you to will and to act in order to fulfill his good purpose" (Phil. 2:12–13). Focus on getting to know God. Pursue knowing Him better through prayer, reading the Bible, and being in fellowship with other Christians. Your faith should not rest in your effort but in God's ability to work in your life. There is a noteworthy quote that says, *"I want to be so full of Christ that when a mosquito bites me, it flies away singing "There Is Power in the Blood."*

Conclusion

We have looked at several tenets of the true Christian faith. While all of them will not develop quickly, they are nevertheless part of the Christian walk. To walk with Jesus is not easy; God does not promise a painless life this side of eternity, nor are we promised an abundance of blessings every step of our journey. Let us remember that God loves us, His grace is always present and sufficient, and most important, He is with us always. This world is not our home. God has planned for His children something so much better than we could ever imagine.

The Bible teaches a person can know if they are still saved by the life they live after they become a Christian. One who is truly saved will give evidence of that salvation because their life will begin to show a tendency toward the things of God and there will begin to be distance between them and the world. The practical reason every believer is to make their salvation sure, is in order to be more productive as a believer.

God has given us the greatest love that has ever been manifested. In return He asks only that we accept His Son by faith, become Christians by following the salvation plan laid out for us in the New Testament (nothing added, nothing taken away), and show our love for Him by keeping His commandments *until the end.* If you want to know that your love for God and others is real, if you want to have the power to obey the commandments of God, if you want to find a life that is loving and not burdensome, then put your faith and trust in Christ and His forgiveness for your sins and His promises for your future. Whoever has the Son has life!

We must live our lives by the Word of God and use the Bible as the sole standard for our guide. We must reject any doctrine, creed, literature, or guides that are not 100 percent in harmony with the Word of God. How can we know we are in perfect harmony? We must study the Bible, learn it, rightly divide it, correctly apply it, and, yes, *obey* it.

As we study the Bible to see if we are in the faith, remember this: the price for being a Christian is high. Jesus set the price for discipleship at a level above the dearest things on earth. He said, "If anyone comes to me and does not hate father and mother, wife and children, brothers and sisters—yes, even their own life—such a person cannot be my disciple" (Luke 14:26). However, we *cannot* reach our goal overnight. James 1:4 says, "Let perseverance finish its work so that you may be mature and complete, not lacking anything." We must however, try for continued growth in Christ, because if you are not moving forward, you are going nowhere!

Additionally, we need a clear understanding of what constitutes saving faith. If we believe in saving faith as though it exists in a vacuum, never yielding the fruits of obedience, we have confused saving faith with dead faith which never saves anyone. Consistent growth and a desire to *obey God* is the evidence of salvation. We must analyze our own lives to see whether we are in the faith (2 Cor. 13:5–6). The big issues here are foundation, motivation, and consistency. If our foundation is the Bible, and our motivation is being like Christ, and if we consistently seek to live like Christ, then we know we are still right with God.

In summary, God wants us to defeat our doubts by placing our faith in the word of God. He wants us to:

- Possess a true sense of inner peace and confidence regarding personal salvation.
- Follow God's plan of salvation laid out for us in the New Testament.
- Continue to grow our relationship with Him through prayer and Bible study.
- Remain Christians and show our love for God by being obedient and keeping his commandments.
- Walk in His path with faithfulness and holding firmly to the teachings of the Bible.
- Use His discipline as a tool to grow closer to Him and remain in submission to him.

The New Testament teaches us that Jesus left Heaven, came down to Earth, was slain and resurrected, so that when we die, and leave Earth, we can live with Him in Heaven. Simply put, God wants us to know Him, honor Him, trust Him, obey Him, love Him, and live with Him forever.

Christ died for us, let's live for him!

"Therefore, my dear brothers and sisters, stand firm. Let nothing move you. Always give yourselves fully to the work of the Lord, because you know that your labor in the Lord is not in vain" (1 Cor. 15:58).

Please direct any questions or comments to:
ecarter4949@gmail.com

Appendix 1:
Summary of the Commands of Christ

- **Repent**

    From that time on Jesus began to preach, "Repent, for the kingdom of heaven has come near." Matthew 4:17

- **Follow Me**

    "Come, follow me," Jesus said, "and I will send you out to fish for people." Matthew 4:19

- **Rejoice**

    "Blessed are you when people insult you, persecute you and falsely say all kinds of evil against you because of me. Rejoice and be glad, because great is your reward in heaven, for in the same way they persecuted the prophets who were before you." Matthew 5:11–12

- **Let Your Light Shine**

    "In the same way, let your light shine before others, that they may see your good deeds and glorify your Father in heaven." Matthew 5:16

- **Be Reconciled**

    "Therefore, if you are offering your gift at the altar and there remember that your brother or sister has something against you, leave your gift there in front of the altar. First go and be reconciled to them; then come and offer your gift." Matthew 5:23–24

- **Do Not Lust**

    "But I tell you that anyone who looks at a woman lustfully has already committed adultery with her in his heart. If your right eye causes you to stumble, gouge it out and throw it away. It is better for you to lose one part of your body than for your whole body to be thrown into hell. And if your right hand causes you to stumble, cut it off and throw it away. It is better for you to lose one part of your body than for your whole body to go into hell." Matthew 5:28–30

- **Keep Your Word**

    "All you need to say is simply 'Yes' or 'No'; anything beyond this comes from the evil one." Matthew 5:37

- **Go the Second Mile**

    "You have heard that it was said, 'Eye for eye, and tooth for tooth.' But I tell you, do not resist an evil person. If anyone slaps you on the right cheek, turn to them the other cheek also. And if anyone wants to sue you and take your shirt, hand over your coat as well. If anyone forces you to go one mile, go with them two miles. Give to the one who asks you, and do not turn away from the one who wants to borrow from you." Matthew 5:38–42

- **Love Your Enemies**

    "You have heard that it was said, 'Love your neighbor and hate your enemy.' But I tell you, love your enemies and pray for those who persecute you, that you may be children of your Father in heaven. He causes his sun to rise on the evil and the good and sends rain on the righteous and the unrighteous. If you love those who love you, what reward will you get? Are not even the tax collectors doing that?" Matthew 5:43–46

- **Love and Pray for Your Enemies and Be Perfect**

    "If you love those who love you, what reward will you get? Are not even the tax collectors doing that? And if you greet only your own people, what are you doing more than others? Do not even pagans do that? Be perfect, therefore, as your heavenly Father is perfect." Matthew 5:46–48

- **Practice Secret Disciplines**

    "Be careful not to practice your righteousness in front of others to be seen by them. If you do, you will have no reward from your Father in heaven.

    "So, when you give to the needy, do not announce it with trumpets, as the hypocrites do in the synagogues and on the streets, to be honored by others. Truly I tell you, they have received their reward in full. But when you give to the needy, do not let your left hand know what your right hand is doing, so that your giving may be in secret. Then your Father, who sees what is done in secret, will reward you." Matthew 6:1–4

- **Lay Up Treasures**

    "Do not store up for yourselves treasures on earth, where moths and vermin destroy, and where thieves break in and steal. But store up for yourselves treasures in heaven, where moths and vermin do not destroy, and where thieves do not break in and steal. For where your treasure is, there your heart will be also." Matthew 6:19–21

- **Seek God's Kingdom**

    "But seek first his kingdom and his righteousness, and all these things will be given to you as well." Matthew 6:33

- **Judge Not**

    "Do not judge, or you too will be judged. For in the same way you judge others, you will be judged, and with the measure you use, it will be measured to you.

    "Why do you look at the speck of sawdust in your brother's eye and pay no attention to the plank in your own eye?" Matthew 7:1–3

- **Do Not Give What Is Holy to Dogs**
  "Do not give dogs what is sacred; do not throw your pearls to pigs. If you do, they may trample them under their feet, and turn and tear you to pieces." Matthew 7:6

- **Ask, Seek, Knock**
  "Ask and it will be given to you; seek and you will find; knock and the door will be opened to you. For everyone who asks receives; the one who seeks finds; and to the one who knocks, the door will be opened." Matthew 7:7–8

- **Treat People as You Want to Be Treated**
  "So in everything, do to others what you would have them do to you, for this sums up the Law and the Prophets." Matthew 7:12

- **Choose the Narrow Way**
  "Enter through the narrow gate. For wide is the gate and broad is the road that leads to destruction, and many enter through it. But small is the gate and narrow the road that leads to life, and only a few find it." Matthew 7:13–14

- **Beware of False Prophets**
  "Watch out for false prophets. They come to you in sheep's clothing, but inwardly they are ferocious wolves. By their fruit you will recognize them. Do people pick grapes from thorn bushes, or figs from thistles?" Matthew 7:15–16

- **Follow Jesus**
  "Follow me, and let the dead bury their own dead." Matthew 8:22

Appendix1: Summary of the Commands of Christ

- **Pray for Laborers**

    "The harvest is plentiful but the workers are few. Ask the Lord of the harvest, therefore, to send out workers into his harvest field." Matthew 9:37–38

- **Be Wise as Serpents**

    "I am sending you out like sheep among wolves. Therefore be as shrewd as snakes and as innocent as doves." Matthew 10:16

- **Fear Not**

    "Do not be afraid of those who kill the body but cannot kill the soul. Rather, be afraid of the One who can destroy both soul and body in hell." Matthew 10:28

- **Hear God's Voice**

    "Whoever has ears, let them hear." Matthew 11:15

- **Take My Yoke**

    "Come to me, all you who are weary and burdened, and I will give you rest. Take my yoke upon you and learn from me, for I am gentle and humble in heart, and you will find rest for your souls. For my yoke is easy and my burden is light." Matthew 11:28–30

- **Honor Your Parents**

    "For God said, 'Honor your father and mother' and 'Anyone who curses their father or mother is to be put to death.'" Matthew 15:4

- **Deny Yourself**

    "Then he said to them all: 'Whoever wants to be my disciple must deny themselves and take up their cross daily and follow me. For whoever wants to save their life will lose it, but whoever loses their life for me will save it. What good is it for someone to gain the whole world, and yet lose or forfeit their very self?'" Luke 9:23–25

- **Despise Not Little Ones**
  "See that you do not despise one of these little ones. For I tell you that their angels in heaven always see the face of my Father in heaven." Matthew 18:10

- **Go to Offenders**
  "If your brother or sister sins, go and point out their fault, just between the two of you. If they listen to you, you have won them over. But if they will not listen, take one or two others along, so that 'every matter may be established by the testimony of two or three witnesses.' If they still refuse to listen, tell it to the church; and if they refuse to listen even to the church, treat them as you would a pagan or a tax collector." Matthew 18:15–17

- **Beware of Covetousness**
  Then he said to them, "Watch out! Be on your guard against all kinds of greed; life does not consist in an abundance of possessions." Luke 12:15

- **Forgive Offenders**
  Then Peter came to Jesus and asked, "Lord, how many times shall I forgive my brother or sister who sins against me? Up to seven times?"
  Jesus answered, "I tell you, not seven times, but seventy-seven times." Matthew 18:21–22

- **Honor Marriage**
  "Haven't you read," he replied, "that at the beginning the Creator 'made them male and female,' and said, 'For this reason a man will leave his father and mother and be united to his wife, and the two will become one flesh'? So they are no longer two, but one

flesh. Therefore, what God has joined together, let no one separate." Matthew 19:4–6

- **Be a Servant**
  "Not so with you. Instead, whoever wants to become great among you must be your servant, and whoever wants to be first must be your slave—just as the Son of Man did not come to be served, but to serve, and to give his life as a ransom for many." Matthew 20:26–28

- **Ask in Faith**
  Jesus replied, "Truly I tell you, if you have faith and do not doubt, not only can you do what was done to the fig tree, but also you can say to this mountain, 'Go, throw yourself into the sea,' and it will be done. If you believe, you will receive whatever you ask for in prayer." Matthew 21:21–22

- **Bring in the Poor**
  Then Jesus said to his host, "When you give a luncheon or dinner, do not invite your friends, your brothers or sisters, your relatives, or your rich neighbors; if you do, they may invite you back and so you will be repaid. But when you give a banquet, invite the poor, the crippled, the lame, the blind, and you will be blessed. Although they cannot repay you, you will be repaid at the resurrection of the righteous." Luke 14:12–14

- **Render to Caesar**
  "Show me the coin used for paying the tax." They brought him a denarius, and he asked them, "Whose image is this? And whose inscription?"
  "Caesar's," they replied.
  Then he said to them, "So give back to Caesar what is Caesar's, and to God what is God's." Matthew 22:19–21

Is it Possible to Know We Are Saved?

- **Love the Lord**
  Jesus replied: "'Love the Lord your God with all your heart and with all your soul and with all your mind.' This is the first and greatest commandment." Matthew 22:37–38

- **Love Your Neighbor**
  "And the second is like it: 'Love your neighbor as yourself.' All the Law and the Prophets hang on these two commandments." Matthew 22:39–40

- **Await My Return**
  "Therefore keep watch, because you do not know on what day your Lord will come. But understand this: If the owner of the house had known at what time of night the thief was coming, he would have kept watch and would not have let his house be broken into. So, you also must be ready, because the Son of Man will come at an hour when you do not expect him." Matthew 24:42–44

- **Take, Eat, and Drink**
  While they were eating, Jesus took bread, and when he had given thanks, he broke it and gave it to his disciples, saying, "Take and eat; this is my body."
  Then he took a cup, and when he had given thanks, he gave it to them, saying, "Drink from it, all of you. This is my blood of the covenant, which is poured out for many for the forgiveness of sins." Matthew 26:26–28

- **Be Born Again**
  Jesus answered, "Very truly I tell you, no one can enter the kingdom of God unless they are born of water and the Spirit. Flesh gives birth to flesh, but the Spirit gives birth to spirit. You should not be

surprised at my saying, 'You must be born again.'" John 3:5–7

- **Keep My Commandments**
  "If you love me, keep my commands." John 14:15

- **Watch and Pray**
  "Watch and pray so that you will not fall into temptation. The spirit is willing, but the flesh is weak." Matthew 26:41

- **Feed My Sheep**
  When they had finished eating, Jesus said to Simon Peter, "Simon son of John, do you love me more than these?"

  "Yes, Lord," he said, "you know that I love you."
  Jesus said, "Feed my lambs."

  Again Jesus said, "Simon son of John, do you love me?"

  He answered, "Yes, Lord, you know that I love you."

  Jesus said, "Take care of my sheep." John 21:15–16

- **Baptize My Disciples**
  "Therefore go and make disciples of all nations, baptizing them in the name of the Father and of the Son and of the Holy Spirit." Matthew 28:19

- **Make Disciples**

    "Therefore go and make disciples of all nations, baptizing them in the name of the Father and of the Son and of the Holy Spirit, and teaching them to obey everything I have commanded you. And surely I am with you always, to the very end of the age." Matthew 28:19–20

- **Preach the Gospel**

    He said to them, "Go into all the world and preach the gospel to all creation." Mark 16:15

Appendix 2:
The Conversions Recorded in Acts

The Ethiopian eunuch heard the good news about Jesus, confessed his belief in Jesus, and was baptized. —Acts 8:26–39

Paul and Silas were unjustly imprisoned in Philippi and were beaten. They used this opportunity to teach the jailor and his household about Jesus. The jailor had a working faith that led him to listen and obey. As a result, he repented and was baptized. —Acts 16:16–34

The Conversions at Pentecost

Peter Addresses the Crowd

Then Peter stood up with the Eleven, raised his voice and addressed the crowd: "Fellow Jews and all of you who live in Jerusalem, let me explain this to you; listen carefully to what I say. These people are not drunk, as you suppose. It's only nine in the morning! No, this is what was spoken by the prophet Joel:

> "'In the last days, God says,
>   I will pour out my Spirit on all people.
> Your sons and daughters will prophesy,
>   your young men will see visions,
>   your old men will dream dreams.
> Even on my servants, both men and women,
>   I will pour out my Spirit in those days,
>   and they will prophesy.
> I will show wonders in the heavens above
>   and signs on the earth below,
>   blood and fire and billows of smoke.
> The sun will be turned to darkness

> and the moon to blood
> before the coming of the great and glorious
> day of the Lord.
And everyone who calls on the name
of the Lord will be saved.'

"Fellow Israelites listen to this: Jesus of Nazareth was a man accredited by God to you by miracles, wonders and signs, which God did among you through him, as you yourselves know. This man was handed over to you by God's deliberate plan and foreknowledge; and you, with the help of wicked men, put him to death by nailing him to the cross. But God raised him from the dead, freeing him from the agony of death, because it was impossible for death to keep its hold on him. David said about him:

>"'I saw the Lord always before me.
>> Because he is at my right hand,
>> I will not be shaken.
> Therefore my heart is glad and my tongue rejoices;
>> my body also will rest in hope,
> because you will not abandon me to the realm of the dead,
>> you will not let your holy one see decay.
> You have made known to me the paths of life;
>> you will fill me with joy in your presence.'

"Fellow Israelites, I can tell you confidently that the patriarch David died and was buried, and his tomb is here to this day. But he was a prophet and knew that God had promised him on oath that he would place one of his descendants on his throne. Seeing what was to come, he spoke of the resurrection of the Messiah, that he was not abandoned to the realm of the dead, nor did his body see decay. God has raised this Jesus to life, and we are all witnesses of it. Exalted to the right hand of God, he has received from the Father the promised Holy Spirit and has poured out what you now see and hear. For David did not ascend to heaven, and yet he said,

"'The Lord said to my Lord:
Sit at my right hand until I make your

Enemies a foot stool for your feet.'"

"Therefore, let all Israel be assured of this: God has made this Jesus, whom you crucified, both Lord and Messiah."

When the people heard this, they were cut to the heart and said to Peter and the other apostles, "Brothers, what shall we do?"

Peter replied, "Repent and be baptized, every one of you, in the name of Jesus Christ for the forgiveness of your sins. And you will receive the gift of the Holy Spirit. The promise is for you and your children and for all who are far off—for all whom the Lord our God will call."—Acts 2:14–39

The Conversion of the Samaritans

Phillip in Samaria

Philip went down to a city in Samaria and proclaimed the Messiah there. When the crowds heard Philip and saw the signs he performed, they all paid close attention to what he said. For with shrieks, impure spirits came out of many, and many who were paralyzed or lame were healed. So, there was great joy in that city. —Acts 8:5–8

Simon the Sorcerer

Now for some time a man named Simon had practiced sorcery in the city and amazed all the people of Samaria. He boasted that he was someone great, and all the people, both high and low, gave him their attention and exclaimed, "This man is rightly called the Great Power of God." They followed him because he had amazed them for a long time with his sorcery. But when they believed Philip as he proclaimed the good news of the kingdom of God and the name of Jesus Christ, they were baptized, both men and women. Simon himself believed and was baptized. And he followed Philip everywhere, astonished by the great signs and miracles he saw. —Acts 8:9–13

When the apostles in Jerusalem heard that Samaria had accepted the word of God, they sent Peter and John to Samaria. When they arrived, they prayed for the new believers there that they might receive the Holy Spirit, because the Holy Spirit had not yet come on any of them; they had simply been baptized in the name of the Lord Jesus. Then Peter and John placed their hands on them, and they received the Holy Spirit. —Acts 8:14–17

The Conversion of the Ethiopian Eunuch

Now an angel of the Lord said to Philip, "Go south to the road—the desert road—that goes down from Jerusalem to Gaza." So, he started out, and on his way, he met an Ethiopian eunuch, an important official in charge of all the treasury of the Kandake (which means "queen of the Ethiopians"). This man had gone to Jerusalem to worship, and on his way, home was sitting in his chariot reading the Book of Isaiah the prophet. The Spirit told Philip, "Go to that chariot and stay near it."

Then Philip ran up to the chariot and heard the man reading Isaiah the prophet. "Do you understand what you are reading?" Philip asked.

"How can I," he said, "unless someone explains it to me?" So, he invited Philip to come up and sit with him.

This is the passage of Scripture the eunuch was reading:

"He was led like a sheep to the slaughter,
    and as a lamb before its shearer is silent,
    so he did not open his mouth.
In his humiliation he was deprived of justice.
    Who can speak of his descendants?
    For his life was taken from the earth."

The eunuch asked Philip, "Tell me, please, who is the prophet talking about, himself or someone else?" Then Philip began with that very passage of Scripture and told him the good news about Jesus.

As they traveled along the road, they came to some water and the eunuch said, "Look, here is water. What can stand in the way of my being baptized?" And he gave orders to stop the chariot. Then both Philip and the eunuch went down into the water and Philip baptized him. —Acts 8:26–38

In verse 36 when the eunuch said, "Look, here is water. What can stand in the way of my being baptized?" all confusion about the medium for baptism should be dismissed. Obviously, the idea of baptism could have come only from Philip's teaching. What did they do? They went down into the water, which conforms with Matthew 28, Mark 16, and Acts 2:38, which we read earlier.

The Conversion of Saul/Paul

Meanwhile, Saul was still breathing out murderous threats against the Lord's disciples. He went to the high priest and asked him for letters to the synagogues in Damascus, so that if he found any there who belonged to the Way, whether men or women, he might take them as prisoners to Jerusalem. As he neared Damascus on his journey, suddenly a light from heaven flashed around him. He fell to the ground and heard a voice say to him, "Saul, Saul, why do you persecute me?"

"Who are you, Lord?" Saul asked.

"I am Jesus, whom you are persecuting," he replied. "Now get up and go into the city, and you will be told what you must do."

The men traveling with Saul stood there speechless; they heard the sound but did not see anyone. Saul got up from the ground, but when he opened his eyes he could see nothing. So, they led him by the hand into Damascus. For three days he was blind and did not eat or drink anything.

In Damascus there was a disciple named Ananias. The Lord called to him in a vision, "Ananias!"

"Yes, Lord," he answered.

The Lord told him, "Go to the house of Judas on Straight Street and ask for a man from Tarsus named Saul, for he is praying. In a vision he has seen a man named Ananias come and place his hands on him to restore his sight."

"Lord," Ananias answered, "I have heard many reports about this man and all the harm he has done to your holy people in

Jerusalem. And he has come here with authority from the chief priests to arrest all who call on your name."

But the Lord said to Ananias, "Go! This man is my chosen instrument to proclaim my name to the Gentiles and their kings and to the people of Israel. I will show him how much he must suffer for my name."

Then Ananias went to the house and entered it. Placing his hands-on Saul, he said, "Brother Saul, the Lord—Jesus, who appeared to you on the road as you were coming here—has sent me so that you may see again and be filled with the Holy Spirit." Immediately, something like scales fell from Saul's eyes, and he could see again. He got up and was baptized. —Acts 9:1–18

"About noon as I came near Damascus, suddenly a bright light from heaven flashed around me. I fell to the ground and heard a voice say to me, 'Saul! Saul! Why do you persecute me?'

"'Who are you, Lord?' I asked.

"'I am Jesus of Nazareth, whom you are persecuting,' he replied. My companions saw the light, but they did not understand the voice of him who was speaking to me.

"'What shall I do, Lord?' I asked.

"'Get up,' the Lord said, 'and go into Damascus. There you will be told all that you have been assigned to do.' My companions led me by the hand into Damascus, because the brilliance of the light had blinded me.

"A man named Ananias came to see me. He was a devout observer of the law and highly respected by all the Jews living there. He stood beside me and said, 'Brother Saul, receive your sight!' And at that very moment I was able to see him.

"Then he said: 'The God of our ancestors have chosen you to know his will and to see the Righteous One and to hear words from his mouth. You will be his witness to all people of what you have seen and heard. And now what are you waiting for? Get up, be baptized, and wash your sins away, calling on his name.'"—Acts 22:6–16

Saul certainly believed in the Lord after his encounter with Him on the road to Damascus. He saw the Lord face-to-face, which allowed him to become an apostle. Did his new faith in the Lord immediately make him a Christian? Chapter 9 says that the Lord

Appendix 2: The Conversions Recorded in Acts

told him to go find Ananias who would tell him what he must do. In Acts 9:18 Saul got up and was baptized. Further, in Acts 22: 16, which is another version of this event, we see that Saul was commanded by Ananias to get up and be baptized for the purpose of washing away his sins. This makes it clear that Saul, who encountered our Lord on the road, was still in his sins at this time.

The Conversion of Cornelius

Cornelius answered: "Three days ago I was in my house praying at this hour, at three in the afternoon. Suddenly a man in shining clothes stood before me and said, 'Cornelius, God has heard your prayer and remembered your gifts to the poor. Send to Joppa for Simon who is called Peter. He is a guest in the home of Simon the tanner, who lives by the sea.' So, I sent for you immediately, and it was good of you to come. Now we are all here in the presence of God to listen to everything the Lord has commanded you to tell us."

Then Peter began to speak: "I now realize how true it is that God does not show favoritism but accepts from every nation the one who fears him and does what is right. You know the message God sent to the people of Israel, announcing the good news of peace through Jesus Christ, who is Lord of all. You know what has happened throughout the province of Judea, beginning in Galilee after the baptism that John preached—how God anointed Jesus of Nazareth with the Holy Spirit and power, and how he went around doing good and healing all who were under the power of the devil, because God was with him.

"We are witnesses of everything he did in the country of the Jews and in Jerusalem. They killed him by hanging him on a cross, but God raised him from the dead on the third day and caused him to be seen. He was not seen by all the people, but by witnesses whom God had already chosen—by us who ate and drank with him after he rose from the dead. He commanded us to preach to the people and to testify that he is the one whom God appointed as judge of the living and the dead. All the prophets testify about him that everyone who believes in him receives forgiveness of sins through his name."

Is it Possible to Know We Are Saved?

While Peter was still speaking these words, the Holy Spirit came on all who heard the message. The circumcised believers who had come with Peter were astonished that the gift of the Holy Spirit had been poured out even on the Gentiles. For they heard them speaking in tongues and praising God. Then Peter said, "Surely no one can stand in the way of their being baptized with water. They have received the Holy Spirit just as we have." So, he ordered that they be baptized in the name of Jesus Christ. —Acts 10:30–48

This is the first recorded conversion of Gentile believers. If we had not read the other examples, a case could be made here that the baptism our Lord commanded in Matthew 28 and Mark 16 is baptism in the Holy Spirit, because this passage states that while Peter was still speaking, the Holy Spirit fell on them. So did this mean they had become Christians? No, the Holy Spirit falling on them became a sign for both the Gentiles and especially the Jews that the gospel was for all. Verses 47 and 48 prove this.

Conversion of Lydia

On the Sabbath we went outside the city gate to the river, where we expected to find a place of prayer. We sat down and began to speak to the women who had gathered there. One of those listening was a woman from the city of Thyatira named Lydia, a dealer in purple cloth. She was a worshiper of God. The Lord opened her heart to respond to Paul's message. When she and the members of her household were baptized, she invited us to her home. "If you consider me a believer in the Lord," she said, "come and stay at my house." And she persuaded us. —Acts 16:13–15

She and her household were baptized.

Conversion of the Jailer

Suddenly there was such a violent earthquake that the foundations of the prison were shaken. At once all the prison doors flew open, and everyone's chains came loose. The jailer woke up, and when he saw the prison doors open, he drew his sword and was about to kill himself because he thought the prisoners had escaped. But Paul shouted, "Don't harm yourself! We are all here!"

The jailer called for lights, rushed in and fell trembling before Paul and Silas. He then brought them out and asked, "Sirs, what must I do to be saved?"

They replied, "Believe in the Lord Jesus, and you will be saved—you and your household." Then they spoke the word of the Lord to him and to all the others in his house. At that hour of the night the jailer took them and washed their wounds; then immediately he and all his household were baptized. Acts 16:26–33

Conversion of Crispus

Crispus, the synagogue leader, and his entire household believed in the Lord; and many of the Corinthians who heard Paul believed and were baptized. —Acts 18:8

Conversion of the 12 Disciples of John

While Apollos was at Corinth, Paul took the road through the interior and arrived at Ephesus. There he found some disciples and asked them, "Did you receive the Holy Spirit when you believed?"

They answered, "No, we have not even heard that there is a Holy Spirit." So, Paul asked, "Then what baptism did you receive?" "John's baptism," they replied.

Paul said, "John's baptism was a baptism of repentance. He told the people to believe in the one coming after him, that is, in Jesus." On hearing this, they were baptized in the name of the Lord Jesus. When Paul placed his hands on them, the Holy Spirit came on them, and they spoke in tongues and prophesied. —Acts 19:1–6

Paul's Instruction to the Romans

What shall we say, then? Shall we go on sinning so that grace may increase? By no means! We are those who have died to sin; how can we live in it any longer? Or don't you know that all of us who were baptized into Christ Jesus were baptized into his death? We were therefore buried with him through baptism into death in order that, just as Christ was raised from the dead through the glory of the Father, we too may live a new life.

If we have been united with him in a death like his, we will certainly also be united with him in a resurrection like his. For we know that our old self was crucified with him so that the body ruled by sin might be done away with, that we should no longer be slaves to sin—because anyone who has died has been set free from sin. — Romans 6:1–7

Please direct any comments or questions to
ecarter4949@gmail.com

www.ingramcontent.com/pod-product-compliance
Lightning Source LLC
Chambersburg PA
CBHW051808040426
42446CB00007B/574